SCOTTISH
TRANSPORT
TOKENS

SCOTTISH
TRANSPORT
TOKENS

RONNIE BREINGAN

The
History
Press

First published 2009

The History Press
The Mill, Brimscombe Port
Stroud, Gloucestershire, GL5 2QG
www.thehistorypress.co.uk

British Library Cataloguing in Publication Data.
A catalogue record for this book is available from the British
Library.

ISBN 978 0 7524 4764 3

Typesetting and origination by The History Press
Printed in Great Britain

Contents

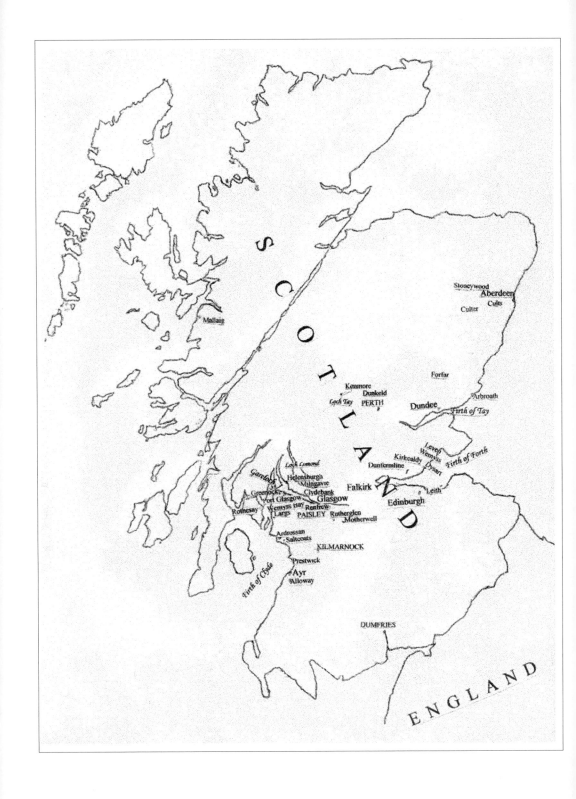

Foreword

By Donal Bateson, Hunter Coin Cabinet

In this age of mass communications we tend to forget there was a time when few travelled far and the horse, ferryman and boat reigned supreme. Then came the stagecoach and the canal boat, the horse-drawn omnibus, the tram and the bus, while larger ferries operated on rivers and around the coasts. Amidst all this hustle and bustle and splendour large numbers of small tokens and tickets played a humble but crucial role.

Ronnie Breingan sets the scene with a fascinating survey of transport in Scotland from the late seventeenth century when stagecoaches were still rare and the sedan chair common. By the end of the eighteenth century roads had greatly improved and canals offered an alternative means of travel. In the early nineteenth century you could travel between Glasgow and Edinburgh by the Forth & Clyde Canal with a stagecoach at either end using a single token. In the cities travel was opened up by the horse-drawn omnibus but in the twentieth century the Corporation transport departments ruled supreme with trams and trolley-buses and huge numbers of tokens.

In a readable and interesting way the development of local transport is integrated into the whole. The various companies are examined and the types, issue and use of their tokens discussed in detail. Tokens were used in cities and towns from Aberdeen to Ayr, where the author comes from; Glasgow to Edinburgh; other cities to large towns. The tokens were produced in aluminium, bronze, brass, and especially plastic in many colours, black to white, and in many shades. Some were for specific users such as telegraph boys, the police and scholars. Designs were simple and gave the basic information required.

The catalogue includes the material, shape, size, description and price. This makes identification of such tokens much easier for the collector and even the museum curator and will be useful to those interested in local and transport history. So often with even quite common types of paranumimatica no catalogue exists yet often much is known about them by dedicated collectors and members of local numismatic societies. Such is the case with the Glasgow & West of Scotland Numismatic Society, of which Ronnie has been a long-time member and past president. The subject was often discussed at meetings but now it is widely and readily accessible thanks to the author and his publishers.

Acknowledgements

I gratefully acknowledge and thank Norman Brodie of the Glasgow and West of Scotland Numismatic Society and Dr John M. Tolson. Both have freely passed on information to me and given me access to their collections. Brian Longworth has helped me with much information relating to the tokens and transport of Glasgow, and introduced me to M. Morton Hunter. Morton Hunter has over many years made a study of the horse-buses in and around Glasgow and has given me a great deal of information on this subject. This includes descriptions of the Rutherglen Omnibus token and the tokens of Wylie and Lochhead.

Andrew Macmillan and Alan W. Brotchie have also supplied me with much information.

Although I was well aware of many of the plastic tokens issued I thank David Stirling for introducing me to the Andrew Menzies copper tokens, in the 1960s.

I thank Mr J.G. Kilgour, formerly of Arjo Wiggins paper mill at Bucksburn, Aberdeen, for advising me about the A.P.S. Stoneywood and Culter Mills tokens. I also thank Iain MacKinnon, personnel services manager of the same company, for forwarding this information.

In relation to the Tay Steamers I would like to thank Keith Mitchell and the Revd Kenneth MacVicar.

I am also grateful to the staff of the Perth Museum; Justin Parkes of the Low Parks Museum, Hamilton; Jane Rafferty and Audrey Cairns of the Documentation Section of Glasgow Museums; staff of the People's Palace, Glasgow; Elspeth King of the Smith Art Gallery and Museum, Stirling; Rowan Brown, formerly of the Glasgow Museum of Transport.

I also thank my son, David Breingan, Dr David Lewis and Billy Fulton for advising me in relation to computer work, and my daughter, Fiona Breingan, and Margaret Watt for reading over the script.

Other members of the Glasgow and West of Scotland Numismatic Society and the Token Congress have been very helpful, including William Reid, who put the catalogue section on to the computer, and Dr Tom Morrall, William Shields and Bill Millar who have helped me over a long period. The society secretary and former president Dr James A. Mackay has also advised and helped me.

Ronnie Breingan

Horse-bus to Tramcar

Most transport tokens in Scotland were introduced in the middle of the nineteenth century but until recent years they did not attract many collectors. The collecting and study of tokens has now very much become a branch of numismatics.

The early tokens were usually struck in brass, copper or bronze but as we moved into the twentieth century celluloid ones were introduced. From celluloid various forms of plastic and fibre have been used as well as various metals. This has continued right up to the present day.

To begin, I would like to think of the days of the stagecoach, the forerunner of many of the forms of public transport which we know today.

There are records of coaches in Glasgow in the middle of the seventeenth century, according to A. Macgeorge in his book *Old Glasgow: The Place, The People 1880*. He states that hackney coaches were said to have been introduced in Glasgow in the middle of the seventeenth century but if this was the case they disappeared again. The book goes on to state that under the date of 15 March 1673 the council refers to 'the provest and to thame he pleases to tak with him, to settle and agrie with ane coach-man for serving the toune with haikna coaches for the best way they can'.

Information regarding coaches in use in Glasgow around this time does not seem to have come to light and it is thought that there were few, if any, coaches in Glasgow for hire or privately owned during the seventeenth century.

In the book it states that Dr Carlyle, writing of the year 1744, says: 'there were then neither post chaises nor hackney coaches in the town. Some sedan-chairs were to be had for hire and a few were kept by gentlewomen of the better classes.' The wife of Thomas Hutcheson, one of the founders of the hospital in Glasgow, is said to have had a sedan-chair. Sedan-chairs were hired out beyond the middle of the nineteenth century.

Stagecoaches, as you may read in the book *Stage-Coach to John O' Groats* by Leslie Gardiner, were in use in Scotland during the eighteenth and early nineteenth centuries. They had to stop, of course, at stages along the route to change horses. Many times they would have their wheels stuck in mud and extra horses would be required to pull them out of trouble.

There were many problems which created high travel costs, although this was certainly a big improvement on travelling by foot or hiring a horse: we have to imagine the distances between towns and villages; the horse rider could be alone over wild open countryside with the possibility of being attacked or meeting highwaymen.

With the stagecoach you did not travel alone. You could even be inside away from bad weather, in a compartment not unlike an early railway compartment. Over the years the comfort of the stagecoach advanced but it still took many hours to complete a journey. There were several overnight stops on the way. This, of course, added greatly to the cost of a journey. Travel was expensive.

People rarely travelled for pleasure during these times. What a difference from today with aeroplanes flying out from the many Scottish airports to different parts of the world! Motorways, express trains, motor-coaches and cars take people to places throughout the United Kingdom and beyond to the capitals of Europe.

Passengers on a stagecoach looked on a journey as an adventure. It was often an experience which worried them so much that they made their wills before leaving.

The condition of Scottish roads at the time added greatly to the discomfort of the coach traveller, although it was two Scotsmen who pioneered the solution to this: Thomas Telford from Eskdalemuir and John Loudon McAdam from Ayr. There is a medal, commemorating McAdam, which depicts his coat of arms.

Thomas Telford was a civil engineer and was born at Westerkirk, Eskdalemuir in Dumfriesshire on 9 August 1757. His father was a shepherd. After school, Thomas was also employed as a shepherd and then he was apprenticed to a stonemason. In 1780 he went to Edinburgh, where he worked building houses. Later he was employed in the erection of Somerset House in London and then he was appointed engineer for the Ellesmere Canal.

He built aqueducts and was engineer for the construction of the Caledonian Canal which was built from 1804, as well as being involved in the construction of nearly 1,000 miles of road in the Highlands and the improvement of the road from Glasgow to Carlisle. He was also involved with roads in Wales together with the construction of the Menai Straits Suspension Bridge and the Conway Bridge.

Telford died on 2 September 1834, after having constructed many more bridges and docks. He was buried in Westminster Abbey.

John Loudon McAdam was born in Ayr on 21 September 1756. He was a Scottish inventor and his development of the surfaces and camber of roads made him famous. Roads used to have pot-holes and the rainwater would lie in them and eat away at the surface, thus making it very uncomfortable to travel on stagecoaches and other coaches and carts.

McAdam's father was a banker who set up a private bank in the name of John McAdam & Co. at Ayr in 1763. The firm was taken over in 1771 by Douglas Heron & Co., the Ayr Bank, which went into liquidation in 1773 with great losses to many local people.

McAdam went to New York in 1770 and worked in the counting house of an uncle. He returned in 1783 as a wealthy man when he bought the estate at Sauchrie, near Ayr. It was on the roads of his estate that he initially experimented. He died in Moffat, Dumfriesshire, on 26 November 1836.

The work of these two men improved and speeded up journeys by stagecoach and the mail-coach which was now on the go.

Down south the mail-coach of a man called 'Palmer' halved the journey time between London and Bristol in 1784 and two years later opened up a service from London to Edinburgh. Many mail-coach tokens exist but the best known are four varieties of the Palmer token.

By the 1820s the stagecoach was big business. From Glasgow to London took fifty-seven hours and from Edinburgh to London fifty-six hours, as quoted in the book *Stage-Coach to John O'Groats*. The same book also tells us how early in the nineteenth century many young boys were coach spotters, just like today we have train spotters. I have also taken from the same book much of the information relating to coaches in the following: the mail-coaches did not have names but all the stagecoaches did. In Scotland examples of these were *Robert Burns*, *William Wallace*, *Mountain Maid*, *Antiquary*, *Rob Roy* and *Talisman*. Perth had its *Fair Maid*; Aberdeen had *Banks of Dee* and Cupar the *Kingdom of Fife*.

Coaches and drinking houses or inns went side by side because people who travelled needed somewhere to stay and eat and drink. Within the 'Second City of the Empire', Glasgow's first coaching house and inn was the Saracen's Head, located off the Gallowgate, which became very well known. It hosted famous people such as Robert Burns, John Wesley, Adam Smith, Mendelssohn, Chopin and many others.

Leslie Gardiner also tells us how much competition and organisation took place in the coach services of the early eighteenth century. In Glasgow strict rules were laid down for the porters and other personnel around the inn yards which were the arrival and departure points for the coaches. These rules stated that no more than six porters were allowed to await the arrival of a coach. They had to stand in line at the kerb of the pavement where they had to wait until a passenger hired them. Porters could not smoke or be intoxicated with drink while they were carrying out or awaiting work. They were also restricted in the charges which they made. It was actually a much sought after and respected job within the city.

Around this time, with competition among the coach firms, many people would travel from Glasgow to Edinburgh by passage-boat along the Forth & Clyde Canal with stagecoach connections to the cities at both ends. This could be done by the purchase of one ticket.

The Union Canal linked Edinburgh with the Forth & Clyde Canal and tokens or time tickets were in use at the beginning of the nineteenth century. These tokens are now rare. They were stamped either 'W' or 'E' for use on the boat heading West or East. They showed 1st, 2nd, 3rd or 4th stage and the time that it would take, such as 1 hour and 55 mines (minutes) for the first stage, 1 hour and 45 mines for the second stage, 1 hour and 45 mines for the third stage and 1 hour and 55 mines for the fourth stage. It would appear that journey times were eventually reduced by ten minutes in each case and new tokens were issued for each stage showing the shorter times.

In those days barges and other boats would travel from one canal to the other by a series of locks. This took a very long time and a lot of effort. In 2000 there was a Millennium scheme to construct what is now known as 'The Falkirk Wheel'. The wheel lifts and lowers boats between the levels of each canal and enables them to sail through a tunnel between each waterway. Tourists may now visit The Falkirk Wheel and experience travelling between the two canals via the wheel.

In about 1830 there were twenty-four mail-coaches on the roads in Scotland of which nine set out from Glasgow. There were in Scotland 316 stagecoaches of which 154 went from Glasgow.

Apart from at the Saracen's Head, coaches left from the Black Bull, the Buck's Head and the Eagle inns. Others left for Perth and Dundee from the Tontine Hotel in the Trongate.

The coaches were for the longer-distance travellers but most people walked around the city. They did not ride horses and rarely, if ever, on carriages although fine ladies would travel on sedan-chairs.

In the early part of the nineteenth century tokens were used on the Union Canal. Boats would sail on the canal from the Firth of Forth and by a series of locks would transfer to the Forth & Clyde Canal and then be able to sail to the Firth of Clyde. Revival and renewal of both canals took place as a Millennium project and The Falkirk Wheel was constructed to lift and lower boats between the two canals.

The Falkirk Wheel is the only rotating boat lift in the world and may be visited throughout the year.

About this time Edinburgh and other towns and cities had rules relating to certain workmen and formed them into societies. These included porters, caddies, sweeps and chairmen. Regulations had to be obeyed and badges were issued and had to be worn by the workmen, just as a number of paupers were allowed to beg and were issued with beggars' badges in some parts of Scotland. The chairmen were the men who carried the sedan-chairs and were often Highlanders.

As time went on, in Glasgow there became many carriages for public hire such as cabriolets, drawn by one horse, from the 1820s. Noddies had four wheels and minibuses had two wheels and they were both on the streets by the 1840s.

Omnibuses ran from the city to its suburbs such as Govan, Partick and Rutherglen but there was still no transport for the ordinary man within the city. In 1845 a man called Robert Frame ran his horse-bus from Bridgeton to Anderston. The charge for a single journey was 2*d*.

Four rivals soon followed with their buses but times were hard. From 1845 there was a great influx of Irish people into Scotland. This was due, very much, to the potato blight in Ireland; because of the shortage of potatoes the price of corn rose steeply. Many people found themselves very poor and hungry. Poverty prevented people from using the new buses as expected and by 1846 all these companies, including Robert Frame, seemed to have failed.

It was not long after this that a man appeared on the scene who was to become one of the most important people in Glasgow's transport. His name was Andrew Menzies.

Menzies was educated at the High School but his interest in horses led him into partnership with a carriage hirer.

Earlier in 1844 in the village of Partick, at that time outside Glasgow, a stagecoach was run to Glasgow every two or three hours for a fare of 4*d*. The firm which ran the coach was Wylie and Lochhead, a name which has been famous in Glasgow ever since, along with their lovely store in Buchanan Street, which is now part of the Fraser Store. To this day Wylie and Lochhead continue, at least in name, to trade as funeral directors and undertakers.

Before the Partick coach, Wylie and Lochhead ran buses to Rutherglen and the Townhead railway depot in the late 1830s. Wylie and Lochhead, whose buses were blue, issued tokens in white metal. They were round with the denominations of 2*d* and 4*d*. The 4*d* token, which was 24mm in diameter, was for use on their omnibuses running to the suburbs and the 2*d*, which was 20mm in diameter, was for more central routes in Glasgow. Both types of token depicted the office address, which was '28 Argyle Street'. The obverse of the tokens showed the name of the company. Because of fare increases and a change in office address about 1857, Wylie and Lochhead issued a second type of token. These new ones were the same as the originals but had the new office address as '58 Union Street'. The denominations were not shown but on the reverse were the words 'Pass Ticket' instead on both sizes. Wylie and Lochhead did later issue welfare tokens. These tokens are brass, round, 29mm in diameter and the denomination was 1*d*. They were probably issued in the twentieth century but not by the omnibus firm, which would no longer be in service by that time.

Another company, which ran buses between Glasgow and Rutherglen, was the Rutherglen Omnibus Co. They issued octagonal tokens in white metal being 26mm by 17mm with the obverse wording 'Glasgow & Rutherglen Omnibus'. The reverse was blank.

Let us return to Andrew Menzies, who was very successful with his buses but had rivals. He had friendly competition from the Walker family, whose omnibuses were brown. They had the Tontine Hotel in the Trongate. Once, when the Walkers were hit by illness, Andrew Menzies managed their business along with his own.

Although Menzies and Walker worked well together, the Rutherglen Omnibus Co. – which was small in relation to the others – did not see eye to eye with Walker. Walker also ran his buses from Glasgow to Rutherglen and was alleged to have reduced the fares so much as to drive the others off the routes and then increase the fares to a higher level. A poster was produced by the Rutherglen company advising the public of the situation.

In 1850 Menzies had nine buses running. Twenty-three years later, on the Glasgow Cross to Anderston route, there was a bus every two and a half minutes. It was said that Menzies opened up Glasgow.

During this period he had another rival, a fellow Highlander named Duncan MacGregor, with whom he did not always see eye to eye. Menzies buses were tartan coloured; they were not painted but tartan-coloured paper was stuck on to the sides and then varnished over as a seal against the weather. They were in the Menzies tartan and MacGregor's were in his own tartan.

Tokens were issued by both Menzies and Walker. By selling a number of tokens the firms were assured of the custom of these passengers. This also saved the conductor or guard, as he was sometimes called, handling the cash. It was therefore, also, a security precaution.

Tokens were in fact the tickets of the time. Paper tickets did not come into use until about the 1880s and in Glasgow on the tramways from the late 1870s.

There were three basic types of tokens issued by Menzies. They were all struck in copper. The first was oval in shape being 28mm by 18mm and had the obverse wording 'Andrew Menzies 10 Argyle St. & 110 London St. 2*d*'. On the reverse was a horse-drawn omnibus and the wording 'City Omnibus', while the name 'Menzies' was on the side of the bus. Some of these tokens exist with a 'P' stamped over the 2*d*. This was to reduce the fare to 1*d*.

Because of changes to the fares new tokens were introduced in 1856. These were oblong in shape, with the corners cut and slight curves on the edge lines. They were 25mm by 19mm and showing on the obverse 'Andrew Menzies Funeral Undertaker and Jobmaster' and on the reverse 'City Omnibus Fare 2½*d* – Jany Glasgow 1856'.

There also exist varieties of these tokens which have the ½ of 2½ obliterated by a countermark to reduce the fare. As a 2½d fare did not last long these tokens were only used for a short time and are therefore quite rare now, whether with or without the countermark.

RUTHERGLEN OMNIBUSES.

TO THE
INHABITANTS OF RUTHERGLEN AND THE PUBLIC.

WHO was it that, on two former occasions, by *Reduction* of *Fares*, Monopolised the Rutherglen Road, and then gave insufficient Omnibus Accommodation, and at once raised the Fares higher than ever?---WALKER.

Who was it that uncivilly used the people of Rutherglen, and said that any thing for them was good enough?---WALKER.

Who is it that is trying the same game again? WALKER.

What were the causes for starting the Rutherglen Omnibuses? Was it not Insufficient Omnibus Accommodation; exorbitant charges when the road was monopolised; and, above all, uncivil treatment? If you wish to have Worse Accommodation; to pay Double Fares; to submit to Insult to Injure your Interests, by all means give countenance to the OPPOSITION.

The Promoters, the Directors, and Shareholders of the Rutherglen Omnibus Company will, no doubt, be guided by the practical response made by the Inhabitants of Rutherglen and the Public.

RUTHERGLEN, 4th October, 1852.

Notice of the Rutherglen Omnibus Co. pointing out to their customers the misdemeanours of the Walker company. (From the collection of M. Morton Hunter)

In 1859 new oval tokens were introduced. These were 28mm by 18mm with the wording on the obverse 'Andrew Menzies Funeral Undertaker Coach Proprietor Glasgow' and on the reverse 'City Omnibus Fare 2*d* May 1859 Andrew Menzies Glasgow'.

All the Menzies tokens are copper as are the tokens issued by James Walker which are now exceedingly rare. There is possibly only one known to still exist. They were issued oblong (28mm by 13mm) with the obverse wording 'James Walker Funeral Undertaker 4*d* Tontine and 104 & 108 West Nile St' and on the reverse is a picture of a horse with the wording 'Post & Job Master Glasgow'.

The tartan buses can often be seen on old paintings of Glasgow. The public found them very colourful.

No known tokens exist of MacGregor's firm but as the others used them it is possible that he did too. They may all have been destroyed or there may still be some lurking in someone's drawer or in the corner of a desk.

Another company running transport during this period and which issued tokens was the Glasgow and Partick Omnibus Co. Ltd. There were three varieties of these tokens struck in brass. Two were round with the wording on the reverse being either 'Half Fare' or 'Inside' while the third type was oval and was for use 'Outside'. These terms, of course, stem from downstairs. In the open-top omnibus being inside referred to being away from the weather, and outside being upstairs, out in the open. The Glasgow and Partick Co. omnibuses were painted in a vivid green.

MacEwen's City Omnibuses issued an oval token (25mm by 20mm). It was a 2*d* token struck in copper. The late Kenneth Smith in his book *Catalogue of World Horsecar, Horseomnibus, Streetcar, and Bus Transportation Tokens Except North America* quotes this token as Glasgow, but the only trace I have of the firm was that a Mr G. MacEwen did set up business with his horse-buses in Manchester in either 1851 or 1852 but that he brought his buses down from Scotland as a readymade firm or company. His buses were in tartan. They were superior in size and comfort to those of his Manchester rival John Greenwood, and Greenwood eventually purchased similar buses from Edinburgh.

In either 1852 or 1853 MacEwen sold his business to Alderman MacKie and so he had only operated in Manchester for a very short time. We are not sure what he did before this or afterwards although it is thought that he had previously operated his bus company somewhere in Scotland. It is highly probable that he issued his tokens in Scotland as he only operated for about a year or two in Manchester.

There are arguments in favour of this being Glasgow: the buses being tartan in colour were like Menzies and MacGregor; Smith's catalogue quotes Glasgow; tokens turn up in Glasgow; the tokens are more in the style of those issued by the Scottish companies. The arguments against Glasgow are: I have not been able yet to trace any record of the firm being in Glasgow; it could have been Edinburgh that he operated in as tokens have turned up there and the buses were probably manufactured there.

Another possibility is that MacEwen worked for Menzies then purchased some of his buses second-hand with the Menzies tartan on them and started up in Manchester.

A copy of an advert and timetable for G. MacEwen's City Omnibus Co. in Manchester exists. At the bottom of the advert there is reference to the fact that omnibus tickets were then available at the office. As paper tickets were not used on buses at that time we may assume that the advert referred to the tokens. This, of course, does not rule out the fact that the tokens may also have been used in Scotland previously.

Most of the information regarding MacEwen in Manchester I have been able to learn from *The Manchester Carriage and Tramways Company* by Edward Gray, published in 1977.

Another company operating in Glasgow around the same time was the Crosshill Omnibus Co. They used small brass tokens each depicting a horse-bus. They were in denominations of 1*d* and 2*d*. The company ran with only two or three buses.

Crosshill was and still is a suburb on the south side of Glasgow although the bus route terminus was at the Queen's Park Gates at the end of Victoria Road. We would now think of this area more as Queen's Park and Crosshill

A horse-bus of the Glasgow and Partick Omnibus Co. Ltd. (Picture from the collection of M. Morton Hunter)

as being nearer to Mount Florida. The other end of the route terminated at Argyll Arcade in the city centre.

The Crosshill tokens are now quite rare but are very attractive in relation to their small size.

All the buses of this period were uncomfortable. Passengers upstairs had the weather to contend with while inside it was stuffy and damp, with smelly straw on the floor on wet days. The public still used them frequently; it was an important form of transport and a good way to get around the city. However, the ride was rough over hard cobbled streets and it was therefore eventually surmised that a smoother ride could be achieved if the vehicle travelled along rails. The result was the tramcar.

Two pictures of the penny token of the Crosshill Omnibus Co. The obverse has the name of the company and denomination. The reverse shows a horse-bus which is typical of the mid- to late 1800s.

The Glasgow Tramcar

At the beginning of the tramcar era local authorities were not allowed to operate tramway services themselves. They could lay the tramlines on their own streets and lease them to a company. After twenty-one years they could buy the company and thereafter operate the tram services.

In Glasgow the Glasgow Tramway & Omnibus Co. Ltd was set up with Andrew Menzies as managing director. After much negotiation this company had to accept conditions drawn up by the Corporation. Under these conditions Glasgow Corporation could after twenty-three years acquire the tramways at one third of the cost or less. The Corporation would lay the lines and the company would pay all the expenses together with interest on the capital outlay.

There were many other conditions, including the plan that the Glasgow Tramway & Omnibus Co. would have a monopoly and run all the buses in the city as well as develop the tramway system.

Other bus firms and companies sold out to 'the Company', which then owned fifty buses and £60,000 worth of stabling for it's many horses.

The first trams began on 19 August 1872. Crowds gathered for the launch of the Glasgow car or 'Glesca Caur'.

Unfortunately in the year after the company was formed Menzies died and, because of the conditions which the Corporation had imposed, all but one of the original directors resigned. The company expanded through the years although there was often disagreement with the Corporation over routes and other matters.

There were tokens of the Glasgow Tramway & Omnibus Co. Ltd. The early ones were both in copper: an oval token stating 'a Letter Carrier in Uniform' and an oblong token stating 'a Telegraph Boy in Uniform'. Both of these were obviously for use by staff in different departments of the Post Office.

There were also other tokens issued by the company. One was brass, 35mm in diameter, round and with the wording 'Glasgow Tramway Co. Limited'. There was a cross pattee with lozenges in the centre and an outer and inner circle of frill design. They were bracteate. The use of these tokens is unknown but they have no monetary denomination and are exceedingly rare.

The other was a sand ticket issued for the staff to collect sand for the cobbles at the rails. This was a brass uniface token with the wording 'The Glasgow Tramway & Omnibus Co. (Limited) Sand Ticket'. This token is very rare.

Aggravation and disagreement continued between the company and the Corporation and on 30 June 1894 the company was forced to stop running its trams. The next morning the Corporation began running their own tramcars on the same lines. The Corporation bought new trams, horses and stables. They would not buy any of the company's stock. The Glasgow Tramway & Omnibus Co. continued to run horse-buses into the Edwardian era.

By this time the celluloid token had arrived on the scene. The company was the first to issue them in the United Kingdom. There were two colour varieties of 1*d* tokens in red and a pinky shade of red.

The Corporation had started with 244 trams and most of the horses came from Ireland. By 1898 electrification had started and soon was extended to the whole system. They built some of the cars themselves.

A horse-bus of the Glasgow Tramway & Omnibus Co. Ltd, May 1894. (Picture from the collection of M. Morton Hunter)

Fares were cheap, starting from ½*d*, so most of the public used the trams to get around the city.

Glasgow became one of the greatest industrial cities of the Empire, and the Glasgow tramway system developed with it, becoming electrified as it moved into the twentieth century.

The trams had different colours between decks to denote the route. This route band was painted red, blue, white, green and yellow depending on the destination of the tramcar.

Tokens were issued by Glasgow Corporation Tramways for the blind. They were struck in brass. The ½*d* was oval and the 1*d* was oblong. Plastic tokens were issued in variations of celluloid, fibre, bakolite and other plastics. They were also issued in a variety of colours. The early ones were issued as Glasgow Corporation Tramways tokens in denominations of ½*d* and 1*d* and varieties of 2 stage tokens. The ½*d* blue and 1*d* white were issued from 1894, when the Corporation took over the tramway system.

Later tokens were issued as Glasgow Corporation Transport tokens in even more denominations; the 1½*d* yellow from 1952 and the 2*d* black from 1953.

Most of those of the 'Tramway' type are much scarcer than the 'Transport' ones except for some of the later 2 stage tokens which are fairly common. A variety of the 'Transport' tokens with the letters J.I.C. above the value exist in the three denominations; ½*d* yellow, 1*d* orange and 2*d* black. J.I.C. stood for 'Junior Industrial Centres' which were centres where the young unemployed were given training in crafts. There was a centre at Dumbarton Road, Whiteinch.

Glasgow continued to issue the coloured plastic tokens well beyond decimalisation in 1971, and even in the late 1990s and into the twenty-first century brass tokens have been issued by First Bus, Glasgow who bought out Strathclyde Buses which superseded Greater Glasgow Passenger Transport Executive and before that Glasgow Corporation Transport.

On 6 August 2005 First Glasgow, which is part of First Group, issued orange plastic tokens of 30mm with the First Group logo printed on them. These were issued on that date only and were given as a promotion to people attending a disco at The Garage nightclub in Glasgow. They were issued to those attending to enable them to travel home free on the night bus service.

I have looked at Glasgow in this chapter, which has given us an overall picture of the development of the transport and the tokens of the period. I would now like to take a trip round the rest of Scotland to take a look at some of the other tokens issued.

THREE

East to Three Great Cities

I have already mentioned the 'Chairman' badges of Edinburgh and the rare Union Canal tokens of the early nineteenth century, but the horse-buses started in the city in the 1850s.

Early rare tokens were those of the Edinburgh Conveyance Co. stating 'Tollcross to Register Office'. These were copper tokens in the denominations of 1*d* and 2*d*.

Tramcars came to Edinburgh in 1871, before Glasgow, and were originally horse-drawn but later they experimented with steam and there were cable cars and those that ran on electricity. There were different companies running the cars and many tokens were issued but mainly in celluloid. Some tokens were marked 'School', 'Exchange', 'Gas Commission', 'G.P.O.' etc. depending on which section of the public required to make use of them.

Lothian Regional Transport, which now runs the company which succeeded Edinburgh Corporation Transport, issued brass tokens until recently.

For the North to Aberdeen line Aberdeen Suburban Tramways issued celluloid 1*d* tokens in black. These are quite rare now. An interesting feature about the Aberdeen District Tramways arose from the fact that in December 1878 the snow and ice put a stop to the operation of the trams and the buses could not cope either. Because of this they introduced what was probably a unique form of transport to the United Kingdom. They began to use sledges which were pulled by four horses. The sledges were simple wooden frames fitted with iron runners on which were mounted knifeboard seats for twenty passengers. No lighting was provided. It is believed that the sledges were only used for a few years as snow-clearing methods improved.

Aberdeen Corporation Tramways, and later Transport, issued many celluloid tokens. Many of these issues are quite scarce today. They also had various colours and denominations including some for ¾d. Like Glasgow the tram system in Aberdeen used route colour bands and also colour lights.

Outside Aberdeen tokens were issued by 'Alex Pirie & Sons, Stoneywood Paper Mills'. The firm subsidised staff journeys from the mid-1850s. The tokens would have been issued for travel on the suburban service of the Great North of Scotland Railway of which the second Alex Pirie, Alex Pirie's son of the same name, was vice-chairman.

There also exist brass tokens with the wording: 'CMP COY LTD – CULTER AND ABERDEEN', and 'CMP COY LTD – CULTER AND CULTS'. These tokens were issued by the Culter Mills Paper Co. for staff journeys on the Great North of Scotland Railway.

From 1854 to 1882 there was an agreement between Alex Pirie Jnr., Stoneywood and Culter Mills Paper Co. whereby Alex Pirie Jnr. had the sole selling rights of paper from Culter. These tokens were in use until the First World War.

Dundee was a city where there were a number of horse-bus operators which issued tokens. John M. Robertson had bronze and pewter tokens showing a horse-bus with the lettering 'Town Omnibus' above. Peter Peebles of Dundee issued a *2d* oblong brass token with the words 'City Bus' and Stratton issued an oval copper token for the 'East End Bus'. Dundee & District Tramway Co. Ltd ran horse and steam trams from 1877 to 1899 when it was taken over by Dundee City

Tramways. Dundee & District Tramways issued brass tokens for 1*d*, 2*d* and 3*d* which are all very rare. The company took over the horse-bus services of both John M. Robertson and Stratton in 1878.

Dundee City Tramways issued many different-coloured celluloid and fibre tokens for ½*d* and 1*d*. These were followed by Dundee Corporation Transport issues of coloured celluloid tokens of denominations ranging from 1*d* to 6*d*. After decimalisation Tayside Regional Transport, which took over from the Corporation, issued 3p orange, 4p red, 5p blue and 10p yellow.

FOUR

Clydeside

From the four large cities let us return west to Paisley where horse-drawn trams ran from 1885 to 1903 and from 1904 to 1923 Paisley District Tramways ran electric trams and issued a hexagonal aluminium token for ½d. This company was taken over by Glasgow Corporation in 1923.

From Paisley there are also rare tokens issued by Spain Gibb & Co. which show 'S.G & Co. Paisley' and are stamped with a number. They are also stamped with either 'EL' or 'LL'. These letters represent either 'empty lorry' or 'loaded lorry' for transport by ferry across the River Clyde.

Around the Clyde there were several tokens issued for use by contractors with vans or lorries such as W Cumming, Cowan & Co., James Shaw, Murdoch & Murray and U.C.B.S., Clydebank, which stands for 'United Co-operative Bakery Service. Most or all of these were for transport of vehicles on the ferries but there are also fairly common tokens issued by Clyde Navigation depicting an anchor and chain. The halfpenny ones are quite common. The twopenny ones are quite scarce while the ones with the wording 'Govan Ferry and Wharf' are quite rare.

A very rare Paisley token is that of The Glasgow & Paisley Canal Co. This is thought to be a trial piece and there are only three of these known to exist.

We now go down the River Clyde to the town of Greenock where there are the rare horse-bus tokens of Murray, James Orr and Donald McFarlane. Two of these tokens show omnibuses while the brass one of McFarlane shows the date 1866. Some scarce celluloid tokens of Greenock and Port Glasgow Tramway Co. also exist.

If we cross the Clyde to Helensburgh we learn of the copper and white metal tokens of Helensburgh and Gareloch Steamers. These were used as tickets on the Clyde river boats. They were return tickets available only on the day of issue and they are all very rare. Incidentally, Helensburgh was the birthplace of John Logie Baird, the inventor of television.

We now go down to Rothesay on the Island of Bute where celluloid and fibre tokens were issued by the tramways. All of these are now very rare. Kenneth Smith, in his catalogues, attributes P.O. Telegraphs Messengers Tokens to Rothesay for use by the messengers as transport tokens. They may have been used in that way at times but these tokens were used throughout the country. I have therefore not included them except for those which are counterstamped with the letters 'RX', which is the telegraph code for Rothesay.

The town of Ardrossan is situated on the mainland further down what has changed from the River Clyde into the Firth of Clyde. The town is known for the pass issued by the Ardrossan Railway. The pass was silver and engraved in old English characters stating 'Free Ticket'.

Around the turn from the nineteenth century into the twentieth century many towns had tramway systems started up or were thinking of beginning tramways. An area of Ayrshire which not many people realise nearly had tramcars was Ardrossan. Plans were made for the Ardrossan, Saltcoats & District Tramways Co. and an Act of 1906 received Royal assent for their construction, but they never did go ahead.

Proposals for Largs and District Tramways extending to Wemyss Bay also failed to go ahead.

It was a very different story in the county town of Ayr. Ayr Corporation ran trams from 1901 to 1931. They ran to their terminus in the holiday town of Prestwick. On the other side of Ayr they ran through the village of Alloway, past Rabbie Burns' Cottage to the Burns' Monument Hotel, now known as the Brig o' Doon Hotel, just past the local parish church and the old Kirk Alloway. There was also a route of single-decker trams which ran to Ayr Racecourse.

Ayr Corporation issued five varieties of celluloid tokens, all of which are now quite rare.

About twelve miles north-east of Ayr is the town of Kilmarnock, which had a tramway system from 1904 to 1931, with trams going out to the village of Hurlford. There are three varieties of celluloid Kilmarnock Corporation Tramway tokens.

In later years Western S.M.T. Co. ran the bus routes in Kilmarnock, where they were based, and in Ayr and many parts of south-west Scotland and Cumberland. Celluloid tokens were issued by the Western S.M.T Co. They are now very difficult to find.

Tokens were also issued by the Central S.M.T. Co. of Motherwell as well as those of the Lanarkshire Tramways Co. and all are well sought after. The Central S.M.T Co. issued celluloid tokens from the 1930s. Some of them appear more like ivory or bone and are smooth with the denominations ½d, 1d, 3d and 1/– printed in black or red while those of the Lanarkshire Tramways Co. are celluloid and depict a double-deck tramcar with the date 1903. The denominations are ½d, 1d, and 1½d in various colours.

Further north and to the east, Walter Alexander & Sons Ltd, who ran the Bluebird buses and coaches based in Falkirk, issued their tokens which were struck in brass and white metal. Dunfermline and District Tramways issued a rare brass type and a very scarce celluloid one in red for the denomination of 2d.

Wemyss & District Tramways also issued celluloid ones in white and green. This Wemyss on the east of Scotland should not be confused with Wemyss Bay in Ayrshire on the west.

One of the rarest celluloid transport tokens issued in Scotland was issued by Perth Corporation Transport. The denomination was ½d and it was green in colour. I have only seen one and it is kept in the Perth Museum. It may be that other denominations also existed at one time and maybe some of them will eventually come to light.

Ferries and Ships

The tokens of the ferries in Kirkcaldy and Leven were used as tickets as were those of some of the shipping companies.

There were the copper tokens of Kirkcaldy or Dysart Ferry showing 'Cabin' with numbers and others showing 'Steerage' with numbers. They were usually round but there was a variety of cabin token which was square. Kirkcaldy, on the east coast of Scotland, was where Robert Adam, the great architect of the eighteenth century, was born. Adam Smith, the economist and writer of the famous and important book *The Wealth of Nations*, was also born in Kirkcaldy in 1723.

There were also copper tokens of the Leven or Largo Ferry showing 'Cabin' and numbers or 'Steerage' with numbers. Some tokens had the letter 'B' and some had the lettering 'St G'.

The round and oval copper tokens of Tay Ferries of Dundee are quite rare and going further south to Leith there are oblong bronze ones depicting 'Leith and Newhaven Ferry' and stamped 'Queen D' in two lines. These are also rare pieces.

With regard to water transport and back to the west of the country, the Caledonian Steam Packet Co. Ltd, which sailed steamers on the River and Firth of Clyde, issued a brass workman's check with the wording on the reverse 'Breakfast Dinner or Supper' shown in four lines.

For longer distances there were the white metal cabin tokens of the Glasgow & Liverpool Steam Shipping Co. They also have numbers stamped on them while on the reverse there is the picture of a steamboat.

The tokens of the Orient Co. Ltd of Glasgow were round and made of brass, stamped with numbers and on the reverse the wording 'Price of ticket to replace this sixpence'. The same numbers appeared on the back and the front. The pieces were holed as issued.

The Subway

There were other ways of travelling around. Glasgow had the only underground railway system in Scotland, and, after London and Budapest, it was the third city in the world to have an underground railway.

Plans were made to build an underground railway in Glasgow in the late 1880s. This system was to be powered by a cable which would pull the cars. The original proposal was to create a service from St Enoch to the West End of the city but this idea was turned down.

After this it was hoped to create a circular system round the west side of the centre of the city with two tunnels going under the River Clyde, but these new proposals were also rejected, mainly because where it went under the river could cause problems if in the future the Clyde was to be dredged and deepened.

In 1889 a tunnel under the river was created. This was a separate venture for pedestrians and vehicle traffic from Finnieston to the south side of the Clyde.

Soon after this permission was given to the Glasgow District Subway Co. to construct the underground cable railway. The Subway, as it became known, opened on 14 December 1896 with a service of twin tunnels, known as the inner circle and the outer circle, and the trains were connected to and pulled by cables. The subway served fifteen stations which from St Enoch were Buchanan Street, Cowcaddens, St George's Cross, Kelvinbridge, Hillhead, Partick Cross, Merkland Street, under the Clyde to Govan Cross, Copland Road, Cessnock, Kinning Park, Shields Road, West Street, Bridge Street and again under the river and back to St Enoch. The total length of the journey was six and a half miles. This was a miniature railway with the rails having a gauge of only 4ft. This, of course, was a very narrow and unusual width between the rails but it served Glasgow well. The island platforms of the stations were only 10ft wide.

At the beginning the fare was 1*d* for any length of journey but into the new century they varied from ½*d* to 1½*d* depending on the length of the journey. Books of tickets were sold in advance at one time but they were really just vouchers which had to be exchanged at the stations for the actual tickets, which did not seem a very sensible system.

In 1914 the name of the company was changed from Glasgow District Subway Co. to Glasgow Subway Railway Co.

In 1916 the flat-rate fare of 1*d* was reintroduced and the prepaid 1*d* tokens were brought into use. The ½*d* token must also have been used around this time as the wording on the token is 'Glasgow Subway Railway' and that only remained the name from 1914 to 1923.

On 1 August 1923 Glasgow Corporation took over the running of the subway. It became part of Glasgow Corporation Tramways Department.

Although there had been several proposals or ideas of electrifying the railway in the early to mid-1920s it was not until after experiments were made in 1932 and 1933 that the electrification of the system took place, in 1935, with the inner circle being converted several months before the outer circle. The Corporation changed the official name from 'Subway' to 'Underground' but the people of Glasgow continued to call it the subway. The original cable cars were converted for use with electricity, and repainted from plum and cream to signal red and ivory.

I can remember as a wee boy during the Second World War travelling with my parents and my brother on the subway. We were on our way home from visiting an aunt who lived in the West End. Before we reached

St Enoch, where we intended getting off, a bomb hit the system and all the electricity went off. The train came to a halt somewhere in the tunnel and the lights went out. I was scared. I do not think that the other passengers, including the adults, were too happy either. We had to wait a long time without knowing what was happening. Eventually men carrying torches arrived. We had to climb down onto the track and walk through the tunnel to the next station. We walked along beside a very high-voltage line wondering if by chance it would come alive again before we could reach the station. We lived to tell the tale and it did not put me off travelling on the Glasgow Subway!

Through the years there were various proposals to improve and extend the underground. During the late 1940s plans were drawn up to add a second circle to the east of the original one. This new rail would also go through the stations of St Enoch and Buchanan Street. This was put forward at the time when Mr E.R.L. Fitzpayne was general manager of the Glasgow Corporation Transport Department. To the east the stations would be in the districts of Gorbals, Dalmarnock, Parkhead, Riddrie and Townhead (plus others). The station at Parkhead is, among other things, a convenient place for visitors to Belvedere Hospital. This is another place which brings back memories of my childhood. In 1943 I was taken to Belvedere Hospital as I was suffering from Scarlet Fever. I was kept in the hospital for about seven weeks. I remember that the building was very old and at night from my bed I could see mice running across the floor. I used to scream for Sister Barr when she was on duty.

One night there was an air raid. I could hear the guns and all the patients were put below the beds for safety. I was only four years old and I had experienced air raids before but I was not used to the mice and, truth be told, it was the mice that really scared me.

With relation to the subway extension, nothing ever came of this or any of the other plans, probably due to the cost of tunnelling. Eventually it was decided to modernise the whole system. It was closed down in 1977 and new tracks were laid. Stations were rebuilt with lengthened platforms and in some cases additional platforms on the other side of the rails. It reopened in 1980 with new trains painted in orange. This modernised underground railway became known as the 'Clockwork Orange'. The old stations and tunnel had a musty smell which was well known to the people of the city, but that was lost when the new trains started.

The main line electric trains through Glasgow Central Low Level and the line through Queen Street Low Level were both modernised about the same time and a new low level station was built at Argyle Street. These lines came above ground on each side of the city and enhanced Glasgow's transport.

During recent years plans were set up to extend the subway system. The proposal was again to create a second circle to the east of the original one. However, due to the high costs it was decided to scale down the proposed extension. Instead of an eastern circle it was decided to employ consultants to enquire into the feasibility of a new line from the Scottish Exhibition Centre, beside the River Clyde, to Parkhead in the east of the city. It was hoped that when Glasgow is host to the Commonwealth Games in 2014 that this new line would be ready for the occasion. There are old Victorian tunnels in Glasgow and it was proposed to make use of some of these in the new venture. Tunnels from the Exhibition Centre to Bridgeton, which are at present used by ordinary electric trains, could be converted for use by the subway, and the old tunnels to Celtic Park in the east and to Yorkhill in the west could again have been brought into service. The new system would also have an interchange between St Enoch Station on the present circle and Argyle Street Station on the present low level railway system. Buchanan Street Station would also have an underground link to the Buchanan Galleries Shopping Centre and to Buchanan Bus Station. Other stations may be modernised and some of their names changed to relate them to nearby museums.

In early times the old Glasgow Subway issued celluloid tokens of ½*d* in blue and 1*d* in white, as I have already given some reference, but it was not until it was refurbished in the 1970s and became known as the 'Clockwork Orange' that a series of brass tokens were issued.

When we think about collectable tokens we tend to look back to the early twentieth century and often to the previous century, but this should not necessarily be the case.

The Glasgow Underground has issued a variety of tokens which are now obsolete and many of them were only in use for a short time.

Shields Road was the first station to use park and ride tokens. These were issued by Greater Glasgow Passenger Transport Executive. They were struck in brass and had the initials 'GGPTE' round a U on the obverse and 'CAR PARK' across the reverse. They were 22.5mm in diameter.

When the transport executive became known as Strathclyde Passenger Transport Executive, a second type of token was issued of similar size and design except that the initials were 'SPTE' with the E reversed. This was obviously an error in striking and was later corrected with a third issue where the E was the correct way round. This new token seems to be less common than the one with the reversed E.

These three types of token were all used at Shields Road Station. When other stations started a park and ride system – Bridge Street, West Street and Kelvinbridge – larger tokens of 24.5mm diameter were used. These issues were of brass and although larger in diameter they were thinner. The wording for each of these stations was different. The Bridge Street tokens had 'STRATHCLYDE TRANSPORT' round a large thin U on the obverse and on the reverse 'BRIDGE STREET PARK AND RIDE'. The West Street tokens were the same on the obverse as the Bridge Street ones but the reverse had the wording 'WEST STREET CAR PARK'. The Kelvinbridge tokens were of the same size but the obverse simply had the letters 'SPTE' across and on the reverse 'K/B'.

At a later date a different design of token was introduced for use at the stations of Bridge Street, West Street and Kelvinbridge. This new type had the same obverse as the earlier Bridge Street and West Street ones but the reverse had no reference to the name of the station and simply said 'PARK AND RIDE' twice. The smaller ones continued to be used at Shields Road Station.

All these seven types of token were eventually replaced with brass ones of 24.5mm. No reference was made to the region, whether Glasgow or

'The Clockwork Orange', Glasgow Subway.

Park and Ride, and they simply had the initials 'ASL' which I assume refer to the company who installed and looked after the mechanism at the car park gates.

Some of these tokens were only in use for a very short time and although quite modern are still scarce.

SEVEN

The Walkers

Another way of getting around the city was, of course, to walk, but even pedestrians did not totally avoid the use of tokens: they were used for bridge passes and tolls. In the centre area of Glasgow there is the Suspension Bridge which spans the River Clyde. In the mid-nineteenth century people were required to produce a special token before they could cross the bridge. These were small oval pewter tokens with 'SOUTH PORTLAND STREET SUSPENSION BRIDGE 1853' on the reverse and the city arms on the obverse.

There were four main passenger railway stations at Glasgow in the mid-1800s. Queen Street and Buchanan Street Stations were both north of the river. They were mainly for traffic to the east and north.

In 1840 trains for Ayr and other towns in Ayrshire started to leave from Bridge Street Station which was on the south side of the Clyde.

The district of the Gorbals was situated to the south of the river. Many of the districts of the city were, in the early to middle fo the nineteenth century, hit by diseases such as cholera and typhus. This situation was greatly improved in later years when water was piped from Loch Katrine to supply the city. This water supply was turned on by Queen Victoria in 1859 and has given Glasgow one of the countries greatest water supplies which has helped improve sanitary conditions.

There were also cotton works in the Gorbals area. One of the largest was the Adelphi Works which was owned by Neale Thomson who also provided a school in Wellington Place for his workers. He lived in Camphill House, which still stands today at Queen's Park. He also had a bakery, called the Crossmyloof Bakery. This was quite a distance from the city centre.

Because of the situation of the railway stations and the fact that many industries had sprung up south of the river, much use would be made of the bridges over the river. For those on foot the South Portland Street Suspension Bridge would have been a great asset.

A recent view of Glasgow's South Portland Street Suspension Bridge.

EIGHT

The Transport Pass

I have tried to look at the various transport tokens issued and used in Scotland but a very closely related issue is the transport *pass*. It is, at times, very difficult to distinguish between tokens and passes.

Passes were often issued for the use of the directors of the companies to travel without payment and often depicted his or her name. Here is one example of a director's pass:

Edinburgh – Round brass pass of 29mm with the lettering 'Edinburgh & Dalkeith' around the edge and 'J. Young' in the centre. The reverse lettering says 'Railway Coach'.

The Edinburgh & Dalkeith Railway started in 1831. It was opened as a horse-drawn railway for the transportation of coal. One part of the track was uphill, through a tunnel and at that part the trains were pulled up by a rope being driven by a steam engine. In 1838 it was extended into the town of Dalkeith. Many different companies and firms ran their trains on this line. A man called Michael Fox converted a stagecoach and used it on the line to convey passengers.

There were many branch lines and they were well used.

By 1840 the main railway company owned thirty-four carriages for passengers. These seemed to be more like early railway carriages. There were no stations at this time so the trains stopped wherever passengers were waiting. Tickets were not used so people just paid a conductor.

The Edinburgh & Dalkeith Railway was once known as 'The Innocent Railway' because they thought that no one was ever injured on it. This was a mistaken idea as there were some accidents and a few people were even killed.

Edinburgh – Round silver pass of 32mm with integral loop at the top and the lettering 'S.M.T. Associated Companies' (around a thistle). The reverse lettering is 'Free Pass' (above a naming panel).

Glasgow – Oval silver pass of 28mm by 23mm with integral loop at the top and the lettering 'Glasgow Corporation Tramways' (on a blue enamel background). The lettering goes around the Glasgow coat of arms which is in silver. The reverse lettering is 'Permit No.' The piece is hallmarked and is by J. & R. Gaunt, Birmingham, 1922.

Ardrossan – 'Ardrossan Railway', engraved in Old English characters. The pass is silver. (Taken from *Tickets & Passes of Great Britain and Ireland* by W.J. Davis & A.W. Waters).

The Clyde – Oval gold pass of 28mm by 18mm and pierced for suspension with the lettering 'Caledonian Steam Packet Co. Limited Director's Pass' and depicting a pennant of the company. The reverse lettering is 'J. Conacher Esq.'.

Arbroath and Forfar – 'The Arbroath & Forfar Railway Co.' is inscribed on a buckled garter, with 'Free/Ticket' in the centre. Engraved both sides on silver. (Taken from *Tickets & Passes of Great Britain and Ireland* by W.J. Davis & A.W. Waters).

Central Scotland – 'Scottish Central Railway Free Ticket'. The reverse lettering is 'Joseph Locke ESQre, Civil Engineer'. Engraved both sides on silver. (Taken from *Tickets & Passes of Great Britain and Ireland* by W.J. Davis & A.W. Waters.)

Great Northern Railway – Oval ivory pass of 30mm by 22mm with the lettering 'Great Northern Railway Free Pass'. The reverse lettering is 'Samuel Mendal Esq. Director M. S & L. Ry Co.'.

Kenmore – Kenmore is the town at the head of Loch Tay where the steamers were based. In 1882 the Marquis of Breadalbane set up the Loch Tay Steamboat Co. This company went into financial difficulties in the early 1920s and was taken over by the Caledonian Steam Packet Co. The service continued until the start of the Second World War when the remaining steamer *Queen of the Lake*, which was built in Troon, was laid up at Kenmore until she was broken up in 1950. Other steamers on the loch over the years include the *Lady of the Lake*, *Sybilla* and *Carlotta*.

A new company was set up and a new steamer was expected to be launched into the loch in 2005. Unfortunately due to problems the new ship was delayed but a smaller cruise vessel, which is similar to those used on the canals of Amsterdam, started operating on the loch in 2005.

It may seem very ambitious to run a steamer service on Loch Tay at the present time. Loch Katrine manages to sail the *Sir Walter Scott*, which was launched in 1900, and Loch Awe has a small cruise vessel.

The *Countess of Breadalbane* sailed on Loch Awe up until 1952 when it was transferred to the Clyde. It must have been in 1952 that my father drove our family down the road between the Firth of Clyde and Loch Awe. I remember it because we came across an unusually wide load: the *Countess of Breadalbane* being transported to her new home where she sailed for many years under that name before being sold to Ritchie Bros and renamed *Countess of Kempock*. She then was transported to Loch Lomond and sailed along with the paddle steamer, *Maid of the Loch*, under the new name, *Countess Fiona*.

Above and below: The new steamer for Loch Tay on the banks of the loch in January 2007.

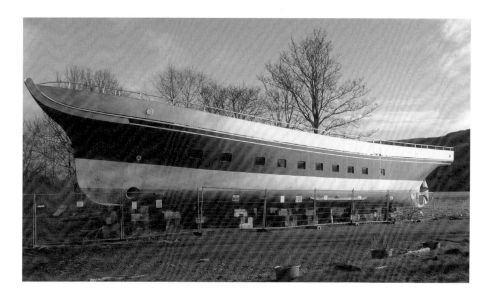

Loch Lomond can no longer support these ships although smaller vessels do give passengers enjoyable sailings. The *Maid of the Loch* is still berthed at Balloch and there is still talk of a fund being set up to restore her. Unfortunately the *Countess Fiona* has been broken up.

In the early 1960s I purchased a Tour Scotland rail ticket and one summer morning I remember reaching the pier at Ardlui at the top of Loch Lomond. I was the only passenger waiting for the *Maid of the Loch* when the man in charge of the pier asked me if I could catch the rope at the bow of the ship and put it over the bollard. I said that I would but I was wearing a light-coloured coat and the pier looked very slippy. When the paddle steamer came in I caught the rope, which was, of course, very heavy and wet. I was trying to watch out that my coat did not get dirty or greasy. I then got to the stage where the important thing was to get the rope over the bollard without me landing in the water. My coat did get wet but I accomplished the task. The man then said, 'That will be twopence for your pier dues'. At least I can say that I tied up the *Maid of the Loch*. I then went on board and had lunch in the ship's restaurant.

Loch Katrine and Loch Lomond are nearer to the cities where most people live, but, never the less, I do hope that Loch Tay does manage to support a steamer service as it did in the past.

Passes were used in the days of the Marquis's original steamboat company. They are of two known types. The first is:

Oval brass of 25mm by 14mm with the lettering 'Loch Tay Steamers around BB' below a crown. The reverse lettering is 'Free Pass' (with a number in the centre). There is an integral boar's head crest at the top and a loop for suspension.

The second is:

A brass oval of 28mm by 15mm with the lettering 'Loch Tay Steamers around BB' below a crown. The reverse lettering is 'Free Pass' on the left, with 'No' (with a number) in the centre, and 'T. Mosley' on the right.

There is an integral boar's head crest at the top and a loop for suspension. These passes were probably given to local workers as well as to directors for their use.

Queen Victoria visited the Marquis of Breadalbane before the steamers were in use and she was rowed up the loch in a small boat. The Marquis's own steam yacht was called *Alma* after his wife. There were also other cargo boats on the loch.

Passes were also used at Wemyss; they were round brass of approximately 42mm. The obverse depicts the lettering 'The Wemyss and District Tramways Company Limited' together with the Wemyss coat of arms. The reverse has the wording 'Service Pass' together with a number. The pass is made of two thin pieces of metal joined together.

NINE

Fringe Tokens

In this chapter I will take a look at tokens with uses on the fringe of the transport scene. These will mainly be tokens which do not have the use of conveyance on a vehicle or other form of transport.

The first group I refer to are pay checks and particularly the pay checks of Glasgow Corporation Tramways and later Transport. These checks were brass and were used to help keep records in the payment of the wages of each employee. There were three basic shapes: the diamond ones were for the drivers; the round ones for the conductors and the oval ones for those at the depots or works. They were all pierced for hanging and had the coat of arms of Glasgow on the obverse, surrounded by 'Glasgow Corporation Tramways'. On the reverse they were stamped with an abbreviation of the depot name and 'DR' for driver, 'CR' for conductor and 'Depot' for depot worker. They all had a number stamped to represent the employee.

As with many factories and works numbered tokens, checks or tallies, as they are sometimes known, would be kept at the place of work. When an employee arrived he would collect his numbered token and keep it with him for the rest of the shift. When the employee left he would then hand it back in. This way a record would exist of who worked each day. It would also show if anyone was late. On pay day, which was usually a Friday, the employee had to produce his token and the equivalent numbered pay packet would then be given to him.

The Dumfries car maker Arrol Johnston issued brass pay checks of 27mm with the company name and a number stamped to represent each employee.

The Glasgow company William Beardmore & Co. Ltd, which was famous for aeroplanes and taxis, issued brass pay checks of 35mm with the wording 'William Beardmore & Co. Ltd' and 'Aviation' and a number stamped. The check was uniface.

'North British Locomotive Co., Queen's Park' was on uniface brass checks with a number stamped on them. They were 34mm and used by the Glasgow company.

There were 'London & Scottish Car Co.' brass checks. They were 32mm with the wording 'Glasgow Garage' and a letter and number stamped on the back.

Also in Glasgow rectangular checks of 29mm by 23mm were used by Rolls-Royce, the aero-engine manufacturer. They were stamped on the reverse with letters and numbers.

The Clyde Shipping Co. in Glasgow had oval bracteate checks or tallies depicting SS *Caledonia*. They were 51mm by 26mm.

Many companies involved in the shipbuilding industry issued works checks. They included:

Clydebank Shipyard which used uniface rectangular zinc checks of 39mm by 29mm stamped with letters and numbers.

Robert Napier & Sons' used rectangular lead checks of 29mm by 20mm and stamped on the reverse with letters and numbers.

Barclay Curle & Co. used uniface brass checks of 32mm with the wording 'Whiteinch' and numbers stamped.

Dundee Shipbuilders Co. Ltd had uniface oval brass checks of 45mm by 26mm.

Other works checks included:

London, Midland & Scottish Railway brass uniface pay checks. They were hexagonal, 32mm by 33mm and stamped with numbers. There were also round ones of 38mm in galvanised iron.

The Peebles Motor Co. Ltd issued cupro-nickel checks with numbers stamped on them. They were of 33mm by 20mm.

Some companies issued canteen tokens. Examples of these are:

Brass canteen tokens issued by the Glasgow Locomotive Works with '3½' in the centre. They are of 28mm.

Brass canteen tokens issued by the Glasgow Locomotive Works with '4½d' in the centre. They are of 33mm.

Brass canteen tokens issued by Wylie & Lochhead (of Glasgow). They are of 30mm, octagonal, with the wording 'Welfare' and '3*d*'.

In Paisley, Carlaw Cars issued brass carwash tokens.
   Other tokens related to transport were brass hexagonal ones issued by the Mallaig Railway Workmen's Club, with a number stamped between 'Member's Ticket'. The reverse had a star design in scores across the brass.

Medallions related to transport include:

A railway medallion in white metal of 49mm and depicting the viaduct on the obverse, with the line 'Great Viaduct Over The Valley of The Almond near Edinburgh to Commemorate the Opening of The Edinburgh and

Glasgow Railway, February 18. 1842'. On the reverse, also with a picture, was written 'Entrance to The Glasgow Railway Station and Tunnel Published by S. Woolfield, Royal Exchange Square, Glasgow'.

A bridge medallion in white metal with the obverse inscription 'Bridge of Dunkeld, Ex Length 685ft. Breadth (sic) 27 and Centre Arch is 90 feet', with a picture of the bridge. On the reverse it says 'Built by the Most Noble John Duke of Atholl. Expence above £30000. Founded 24th June 1805 and Opened the 7th Novr 1808'.

A silver medallion of the Dunvegan Castle Steam Ship with the obverse showing the ship within a life belt, inscribed 'Sports on Board Castle Cos. Steamer' (all shown upon an anchor with olive branches at side). On the reverse '2nd Prize Dunvegan Castle' has been engraved.

A gilt-bronze uniface medallion showing the The George Bennie Rail Plane on a monorail, above a steam locomotive. Below is the wording 'Opening June 1930'. It is 27mm and has a ring for suspension. This rail plane was at Milngavie, Glasgow, where a short experimental section was built. Although the structural work which was required for the rail plane to run on, above ground level, appeared expensive to construct, Bennie maintained that the construction costs would be less than an ordinary railway as the cost of ground clearance and other expenses would be less. Unfortunately, the rail plane and construction were scrapped in 1956.

The tokens listed in this chapter are in no way a comprehensive list of all the tokens, checks or medallions relating to the fringe of transport tokens of Scotland but should be treated as examples of the many that do exist or have existed.

Colourful Cities

Through the years transport has created many colourful scenes on the streets of Glasgow. In the past there were many brightly decorated horse-bus companies and firms that ran routes in the centre and suburbs of the city. The ones that I know which issued tokens I have mentioned.

Tokens were in early days the form of tickets. They could be purchased beforehand and it saved the conductor, or guard as he was better known, handling actual cash. It was not until about the 1880s that paper tickets were generally used although, I believe, the Glasgow Tramway & Omnibus Co. did issue paper tickets from the 1870s. Tokens were sometimes issued at a discount for say, thirteen penny tokens for one shilling.

As I only know of one Walker token having survived the Victorian times and I have only heard of one or two of the Rutherglen Omnibus firm and one of each of the four types of Wylie & Lochhead Omnibus tokens surviving, I am sure that it would be correct to assume that many of the smaller companies also issued tokens. I think therefore that over the years most of these tokens have found their way into waste bins. It is always possible that one or two of them may have survived and still turn up.

If we had been walking on the streets of the city from the 1850s onward we would have noticed that the horse-buses of Andrew Menzies were all decorated on their sides in the Menzies tartan and those of MacGregor were in the MacGregor tartan.

The buses of Wylie & Lochhead were painted blue while those of Walker were brown. Glasgow & Partick Omnibus Co. chose a vivid green. The Thomas Blair buses from 1884 to 1896 were also green. This is, of course, one of the many companies for which we have no trace of token usage.

Some people may say that the tokens would probably have only been issued by the larger companies. This, though, is not the case. Crosshill Omnibus Co. only had two or three buses and Rutherglen Omnibus Co. probably had even fewer. I often think that Burnside Omnibus Co., which was based near Rutherglen, would probably have issued tokens like the Rutherglen company. M. Morton Hunter, in his studies of the Glasgow horse-bus, has also mentioned companies and firms such as Thomas Craig (in 1857), Robertson's 'Kelvindock Omnibus', the 'Shaw bus', John Mercer, Crawford, George Watson, James Frazer, Willie Dunlop, Matthew Cook and Charles Cook, William Govan, John Russell, John Bennie of Parkhead and many more. I think that these are mainly smaller companies but there is no reason to think that many of them did not use tokens.

When the Glasgow Tramway & Omnibus Co. was formed they used colours on their trams to denote the route which the car was taking. The colours were under the lower saloon windows. They consisted of yellow, green, blue, red, two shades of brown, white and the Menzies tartan. The streets of Glasgow, therefore, continued to remain colourful.

The Glasgow Corporation continued to use some of the route colours. They were yellow, green, blue, red and white, but they were by this time on the upper panels above the lower deck windows with crimson lake, a shade of maroon, on the lower panels.

After the Corporation took over the tramway the Glasgow Tramway & Omnibus Co. continued to run horse-buses in the city and suburbs and they were painted brown with no route colour. The company also ran their buses in Edinburgh and Leith about this time.

M. Morton Hunter tells us that on 29 September 1894 Glasgow Corporation began to run horse-buses. They were small double-deckers which they used as feeders to the tram routes. They were painted in crimson lake and cream.

Just before the turn of the century Glasgow Corporation began the electrification of the tramway system. The first electric trams were single-deckers, with two saloons and doors in the middle. The panels below the windows were coloured cadmium yellow. This is a light shade of orange and although it continued throughout the life of the Glasgow tram it was slightly darkened in later years. From the beginning of the electrification the double-decker trams had the upper panels in the route colours the same as the horse-drawn ones.

Glasgow Corporation began the motorbus service in 1924 with single-deckers. The original colour was to be ultra-marine but they were actually painted orange and cream. Double-deckers came into service in 1928 and were painted green, orange and cream. The green was slightly lighter than the green route bands on the trams and became known as 'bus green'.

Eventually route numbers were introduced for the buses and later the colours on the trams were replaced by route numbers.

When I was young, and before I could read, there were basically three bus routes which I used with my parents and my brother. The first of these was the 4A from Croftfoot to Govan Cross, which we often used to go to Shawlands. The number 5 had variations of the route called 5A, 5B and 5C. We used these variations to go to town or the West End. Lastly there was also the number 13, which we used to go to the more eastern end of the town or to go to the Florida cinema.

Although I could not read I knew which bus was coming as all the 4A buses ran on gas. Because of fuel shortages during the Second World War gas was used to propel some vehicles. All the 4A buses had a trailer behind them which produced the gas. I well remember how these buses often got stuck on the Menock Road hill.

The route 13 buses were all Albions and therefore their engines had a distinctive sound which I could identify. All other buses were therefore on the number 5 route.

One evening during the Second World War my parents, my brother and I were travelling from the West End, where we had been visiting relatives. Our bus was near Larkfield Garage when there was an air raid. The driver drove into the garage and we all stepped off and were taken down below ground past pipes and a tank, which could have been used to carry oil or petrol. I think we felt that we would have been safer above ground!

I also visited the garage in the 1950s. My brother, myself and another boy were shown round the premises including the bus works. We had a great time and we saw what I called the 'Big Long Bus'. This was number 238, a three-axled, six-wheeled AEC double-decker. We were told that this was the only six-wheeler used by Glasgow Corporation. This surprised me as I thought that there were several. I must have seen the same bus at many different places throughout the years. There was a demonstrator Leyland with six wheels which was used in 1933. This bus was in Glasgow Corporation colours but ran in Glasgow many years before I was born, so I was not confusing this with the AEC.

Variations of the bus colours continued throughout the years and when the modern 'Coronation Tramcars' appeared in the late 1930s the first one was painted in red, silver and blue. All these new trams were then painted in similar colours to the buses.

The white and green standard car route colours were phased out and replaced with bus green by 1942. The other route colours were replaced with bus green by mid-1950. There had been an attempt to reintroduce the original colours in 1949 when a small number of 'Coronation' and 'Curnarder' cars were given red route colours, but this did not last long. The first time I fully realised that the route colours were no longer used was one day when I was waiting at a bus stop just outside Langside Tramway Depot. I saw the tramcars in the depot and away at the back I saw two trams with coloured route bands. All the rest were bus green. I realised that these two trams were no longer used in service and that the colourful custom in Glasgow was gone.

In 1947 an experimental tram with separate entrance and exit appeared on the streets of Glasgow. This was a magnificent tramcar in three shades of blue. It was eventually altered into a conventional style and painted in bus colours.

Glasgow Corporation Transport was colourful but there were also small single-deck grey buses which could be seen on the streets of the city and around the suburbs. These buses were run by Glasgow Corporation Education Department and not much has been written about them. They were used to take children to and from 'Special Schools' and they were also used to deliver school dinners.

I can remember seeing these buses and my recollection is of small flat-fronted vehicles with the radiators at the front. I seem to remember them being Albions. I know that some of them were also half cabs and that the early buses had the earlier style of bonnets protruding out on front. They seemed to stay in service until the mid-1970s when they were replaced by blue and cream buses of Strathclyde Region. Some people say that these grey buses were garaged near the Old Town Hall in Govan.

In the 1950s there was a fruitman, named Tommy, who sold his fruit and vegetables from an old bus in the Croftfoot area in the south side of Glasgow. I used to get a lift for a short spell on Tommy's old bus. It was painted blue and I think that the registration number included the letters 'GE' or something similar. The registration was not that of one of the early Glasgow Corporation route buses but as this vehicle was quite short I wonder now if it could have been a former Education Department bus painted blue over the grey. Tommy did not own the business. I think it was owned by someone called Docherty. If the bus was not originally one of the grey ones it must certainly have been owned and run by one of the early motor bus companies.

Many companies ran motorbuses in and around Glasgow during the early part of the first half of the twentieth century. The buses were of various colours, including the blue Pullman ones of Harold Whatmough.

Greater Glasgow Passenger Transport Executive bus numbered L 108, with the registration number SGD 10, after it was converted to an 'open top'. The bus was originally run by Glasgow Corporation Transport.

Rankin Bros were beige and ran to the outskirts of the city to places like Cumbernauld and East Kilbride. East Kilbride was not much more than a village in those days. In the 1950s I used to cycle from Croftfoot in Glasgow to East Kilbride, where they were starting to build the new town. The construction of roundabouts was very obvious, with cycle tracks running underneath. I thought that it was very modern at the time. This was the beginning of the creation of the 'roundabout town' of Scotland.

From 1926 the Glasgow General Omnibus Co. operated red and cream single-deckers. They ran to towns such as Hamilton, Uddingston, Dalmuir, Falkirk, Balloch and East Kilbride. From 1929 they changed their livery to blue and cream and double-deckers were introduced.

1. Reverse – Andrew Menzies 2d depicting a horsebus. (Ref RB 294)
2. Obverse – Andrew Menzies 2d. (Ref RB 294)
3. Obverse – Andrew Menzies 2d, 1859. (Ref RB 298)
4. Reverse – Andrew Menzies 2d, 1859. (Ref RB 2984)
5. Obverse – James Walker 4d. (Ref RB 290)
6. Reverse – James Walker 4d. (Ref RB 290)
7. Reverse – Crosshill Omnibus (horsebus)
8. Obverse – Crosshill Omnibus 1d. (Ref RB 301)
9. Obverse – Andrew Menzies 2½d, 1856. (Ref RB 296)
10. Reverse – Andrew Menzies 2½d, 1856. (Ref RB 296)
11. Obverse – MacEwens 2d. (Ref RB 285)
12. Reverse – MacEwens 2d. (Ref RB 285)
13. Obverse – The Glasgow Tramway & Omnibus Co. Ltd. (Ref RB 308)

14. Reverse – Letter carrier in uniform. (Ref RB 308)
15. Obverse – The Glasgow Tramway & Omnibus Co. Ltd.
    (Ref RB 309)
16. Reverse – Telegraph boy in uniform. (Ref RB 309)
17. Obverse – Glasgow Tramway Co. Ltd. (Ref RB 305)
18. Obverse – Glasgow Tramway & Omnibus Co. Ltd Sand Ticket.
    (Ref RB 306)
19. Reverse – The Glasgow Tramway & Omnibus Co. Ltd 1d
    (celluloid). (Ref RB 355)
20. Obverse – Celluloid – depicting tramcar. (Ref RB 355)
21. Obverse – Glasgow Corporation Tramways 1d (oblong). (Ref RB 345)
22. Reverse – Blind (oblong). (Ref RB 345)
23. Obverse – Glasgow Corporation Tramways ½d (oval). (Ref RB 344)
24. Reverse – Blind (oval). (Ref RB 344)
25. Obverse – Glasgow Subway Railway (celluloid). (Ref RB 350)
26. Reverse – ½d. (Ref RB 350)

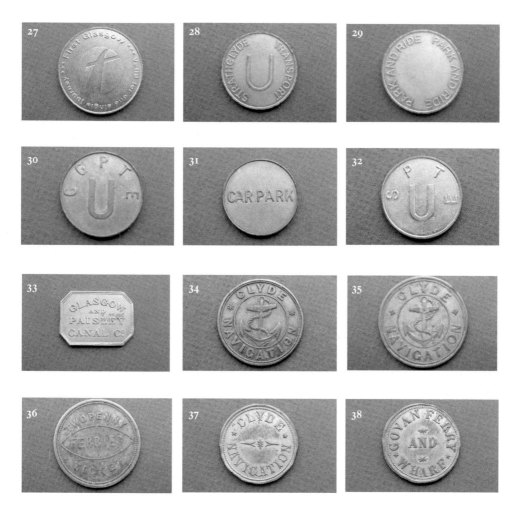

27. Obverse – First Glasgow. (Ref RB 435)
28. Obverse – Strathclyde Underground Park & Ride.
    (Ref RB 556)
29. Reverse – Strathclyde Underground Park & Ride.
    (Ref RB 556)
30. Obverse – Greater Glasgow Passenger Transport Executive,
    Underground Park & Ride. (Ref RB 550)
31. Reverse – Greater Glasgow Passenger Transport Executive,
    Underground Park & Ride. (Ref RB 550)
32. Obverse – Strathclyde Passenger Transport Executive Underground Park & Ride. (Ref RB 551)
33. Obverse – Glasgow and Paisley Canal Co. (Ref RB 321)
34. Obverse – Clyde Navigation ½d ferries. (Ref RB 327)
35. Obverse – Clyde Navigation 2d ferries. (Ref RB 326)
36. Reverse – Clyde Navigation 2d ferries. (Ref RB 326)
37. Obverse – Clyde Navigation, Govan ferry and wharf. (Ref RB 325)
38. Reverse – Clyde Navigation, Govan ferry and wharf. (Ref RB 325)
39. Obverse – United Co-operative bakeries, Renfrew Ferry. (Ref RB 84)

40. Obverse – W. Cumming. (Ref RB 506)

41. Obverse – Jas Shaw, contractor. (Ref RB 365)

42. Obverse – M/M Ferry. (Ref RB 515)

43. Obverse – Cowan & Co., Ferry. (Ref RB 312)

44. Obverse – R.D.S. Ltd, Ferry. (Ref RB 338)

45. Reverse – South Portland Street Suspension Bridge, 1853. (Ref RB 440)

46. Obverse – South Portland Street Suspension Bridge, 1853. (Ref RB 440)

47. Obverse – Glasgow & Partick Omnibus Co. Ltd, inside. (ref RB 281)

48. Reverse – Glasgow & Partick Omnibus Co. Ltd, inside. (ref RB 281)

49. Obverse – Glasgow & Partick Omnibus Co. Ltd, half-fare. (Ref RB 280)

50. Reverse – Glasgow & Partick Omnibus Co. Ltd, half-fare. (Ref RB 280)

51. Obverse – Gold Pass – Caledonian Steam packet Co. Ltd. (Ref RB 640)

52. Reverse – Gold Pass – Caledonian Steam packet Co. Ltd. (Ref RB 640)

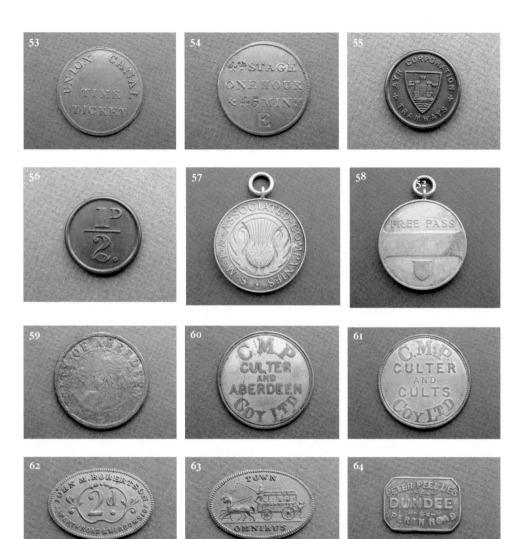

53. Obverse – Union Canal Time Ticket. (Ref RB 177)
54. Reverse – Union Canal Time Ticket. (Ref RB 177)
55. Obverse – Ayr Corporation Tramways ½d. (Ref RB 80)
56. Reverse – Ayr Corporation Tramways ½d. (Ref RB 80)
57. Obverse – Silver Pass – SMT & Associated Companies.
   (Ref RB 610)
58. Reverse – Silver Pass – SMT & Associated Companies.
   (Ref RB 610)
59. Obverse – Aberdeen Sand. (Ref RB 1)
60. Obverse – CMP Coy Ltd, utler and Aberdeen. (Ref RB 87)
61. Obverse – CMP Coy Ltd, Culter and Cults. (Ref RB 88)
62. Obverse – John M. Robertson (Dundee) 2d. (Ref RB 90)
63. Reverse – John M. Robertson (Dundee) 2d. (Ref RB 90)
64. Obverse – Peter Peebles, Dundee 2d. (Ref RB 94)
65. Reverse – Peter Peebles, Dundee 2d. (Ref RB 94)

66. Obverse – Stratton 2*d* (Dundee). (Ref RB 96)

67. Reverse – Stratton 2*d* (Dundee) East End bus. (Ref RB 96)

68. Obverse – Edinburgh Conveyance Co. 2*d*. (Ref RB 186)

69. Reverse – Edinburgh Conveyance Co. 2*d*. Tollcross to Register Office. (Ref RB 186)

70. Obverse – London & Edinburgh Shipping Co. Ltd. (Ref RB 182)

71. Obverse – Lothian Regional Transport. (Ref RB 265)

72. Obverse – W. Alexander & Sons, Falkirk, 2½. (Ref RB 273)

73. Obverse – James Orr, Greenock. (Ref RB 452)

74. Reverse – James Orr, Greenock. (Ref RB 452)

75. Obverse – Donald McFarlane, Greenock 2*d*, 1866. (Ref RB 454)

76. Reverse – Donald McFarlane, Greenock 2*d*, 1866. (Ref RB 454)

77. Obverse – Helensburgh and Gareloch steamers return ticket. (Ref RB 464)

78. Reverse – Helensburgh and Gareloch steamers return ticket. (Ref RB 464)

79. Obverse – Helensburgh and Gareloch steamers pattern.
(Ref RB 467)

80. Obverse – Kirkcaldy or Dysart Ferry. (Ref RB 476)

81. Obverse – Pass – Loch Tay steamers. (Ref RB 680)

82. Reverse – Pass – Loch Tay steamers. (Ref RB 680)

83. Obverse – Mallaig Railway Workmen's Club. (Ref RB 1000)

84. Obverse – Spain Gibb & Co. of Paisley (for empty lorry).
(Ref RB 502)

85. Obverse – Spain Gibb & Co. of Paisley (for loaded lorry).
(Ref RB 503)

86. Obverse – Paisley District tramways Co. ½d. (Ref RB 500)

87. Reverse – Paisley District tramways Co. ½d. (Ref RB 500)

88. Obverse – Aberdeen Corporation Tramways ½d. (Ref RB 37)

89. Reverse – Aberdeen Corporation Tramways ½d. (Ref RB 37)

90. Obverse – Dundee City Tramways 1d. (Ref RB 118)

91. Reverse – Dundee City Tramways 1d. (Ref RB 118)

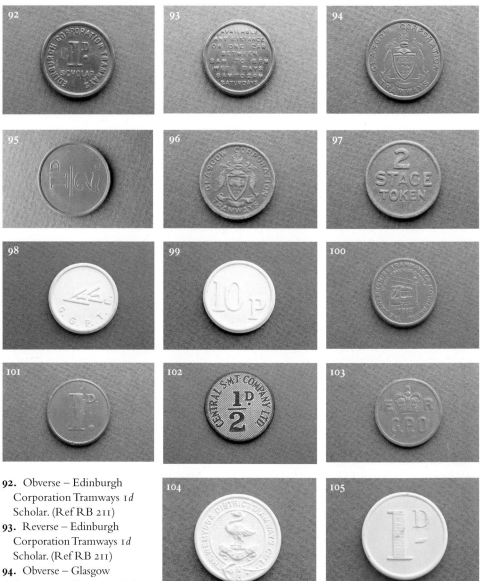

92. Obverse – Edinburgh
    Corporation Tramways 1*d*
    Scholar. (Ref RB 211)
93. Reverse – Edinburgh
    Corporation Tramways 1*d*
    Scholar. (Ref RB 211)
94. Obverse – Glasgow
    Corporation Tramways ½*d*.
    (Ref RB 377)
95. Reverse – Glasgow
    Corporation Tramways ½*d*. (Ref RB 377)
96. Obverse – Glasgow Corporation Tramways 2 Stage Token in fibre. (Ref RB 393)
97. Reverse – Glasgow Corporation Tramways 2 Stage Token in fibre. (Ref RB 393)
98. Obverse – Greater Glasgow Passenger Transport Executive 10p. (Ref RB 431)
99. Reverse – Greater Glasgow Passenger Transport Executive 10p. (Ref RB 431)
100. Obverse – The Lanarkshire Tramways Co. 1*d*. (Ref RB 489)
101. Reverse – The Lanarkshire Tramways Co. 1*d*. (Ref RB 489)
102. Obverse – Central S.M.T. Co. (of Motherwell) ½*d*. (Ref RB 494)
103. Reverse – Rothesay Tramways G.P.O. token. (Ref RB 520)
104. Obverse – Wemyss & District Tramways Co. Ltd 1*d*. (Ref RB 530)
105. Reverse – Wemyss & District Tramways Co. Ltd 1*d*. (Ref RB 530)

The company became Central S.M.T. Co. from 1932. Central S.M.T. issued plastic tokens, in denominations of ½*d*, 1*d*, 3*d* and 1/-. These tokens had printed figures and wording on them and they were therefore quite liable to wear. In some cases their plastic looked like ivory.

Other companies such as O'Hara's had yellow buses while Sanderson Brothers had dark blue and there was the Red Bus Service of Bain and Laird of Kikintilloch.

Many other companies ran local services in and out of Glasgow. As I have said, many of the other horse-bus companies would issue tokens but I am not convinced that the smaller motorbus companies used them. Tickets were very much on the go by that time and I am sure that many of the smaller concerns would not bother to use tokens. Some of these buses used to race each other to pick up the passengers.

There were also a number of companies which ran long-distance services from Glasgow. These included, from 1927, Marley's Anglo-Scots Motorways with coaches which were yellow with black roofs. From 1929 there were blue coaches curtesy of Gordon Bros County Motor Services , which was based in Stakeford, Northumberland, but ran the route from Glasgow to Newcastle via Edinburgh. From 1927 Clan Motorways of Glasgow ran the Aberdeen service. Their luxury coaches were blue with a narrow band of tartan below the windows. This was a reminder of the old Menzies and MacGregor tartan horse-bus days. Even though Clan Motorways ran this service in the 1920s you could travel in a coach with an observation section and a toilet. More recently the London route was served by the black and white coaches of Western S.M.T., which issued plastic tokens, but I am sure these tokens were not intended for the long-distance routes. Among the other companies which ran routes to London were Northern Roadways, Cotters and, of course, Stagecoach.

During the twentieth century, and for a short time before it, the tokens issued in Glasgow had become the type made of celluloid or plastic and like the vehicles they were in a great variety of colours.

I remember when I was in my early teens going to my grandparents' home in Pollokshields in a yellow tramcar on the number 12 route. I was sitting upstairs, right at the front. After giving the conductress money for my fare she said that she had no change and asked if I would mind taking tokens instead of money. I was pleased to accept the variety of coloured plastic money. This was not my first encounter with tokens but it is certainly the one I remember best. I am sure this must have had an influence on the fact that I later collected them. Another influence has certainly been that I became a numismatist and I eventually related the collecting of coins with the collecting of tokens.

Glasgow's trams, buses and, from their introduction in 1949, trolleybuses continued in variations of the bus colours until in the 1970s the Greater Glasgow Passenger Transport Executive took over the assets of Glasgow Corporation Transport. The trams made their last run on 4 September 1962 and the short life of the trolleybuses ended on 28 May 1967.

Under the Greater Glasgow Passenger Transport Executive buses appeared in green, white and yellow, which was in many ways a variation of the Glasgow Corporation colours except that the green was darker and below the lower deck windows. The yellow was below the windows of the upper deck, with a white roof and white window surrounds. The name was changed in 1980 to Strathclyde Passenger Transport Executive. The Greater Glasgow Passenger Transport Executive issued plastic tokens worth 5p (black) and 10p (white) with a large GG logo in the centre of the obverse side.

Eventually the buses were painted 'Strathclyde Red', which was really a dark orange, and the company was now named Strathclyde Buses. Gradually the colour of the buses was changed to red and the company was taken over by First Group which changed them to their standard livery we see today: reddish pink, and a purple shade comprising of blue and white. The company has discontinued the old Corporation numbering system for each bus and now number them according to their national numbering system.

I am pleased to say that First Bus, or as it is known locally First Glasgow, issue brass tokens. These may be used for one single journey of any length at any time of day and on any day of the week. The original versions of these tokens were struck by the Birmingham mint but new ones of the

Bus in the colours of the Greater Glasgow Passenger Transport Executive. The bus is numbered AV 1 with the registration number GGG 300N. This photo was taken at Larkfield Garage.

same design were struck at St Paul's Mint, York, in 2006. Orange plastic ones with the First Bus logo printed on them were issued for a night service promotion and were only valid during the early hours of Saturday 6 August 2005. They were issued for patrons of The Garage nightclub.

ELEVEN

Coach Builders

In Edinburgh we can look back to an earlier period when stagecoaches were running to and from the city. Not only were the coaches known to follow their own routes but Edinburgh became a city which was famous throughout Europe for the manufacture of high-quality stagecoaches.

In the eighteenth century a man called John Home built stagecoaches in a way that had never been done before. He employed men who each concentrated on a particular part of the coach such as specific panels or the roof. With this method his employees quickly became experts in their particulr area of work The vehicles were of a very high quality and levels of production were high.

Edinburgh became the centre for stagecoach manufacture and its coaches were exported to many parts of Europe and beyond.

Other great names of stagecoach building in Edinburgh were Croall and McNee, both of whom were among the largest builders of coaches in Great Britain.

As Edinburgh went into the nineteenth century there were many horse-bus operators. Even steam buses and carriages appeared. As early as 1827 a man called James Nasmyth ran a steam bus. There was more interest in steam-propelled buses in the 1860s. A Mr A. Ritchie who ran horse-buses decided to try steam power by pulling a trailer, designed for passengers, behind a steam engine. Other operators used steam buses around the early 1870s but as they were required to have a boy walk in front of them with a red flag they eventually disappeared although, of course, the use of horse-buses continued.

From 1869 the horse-buses on each particular route in Edinburgh were required to be painted in a specific colour, even though more than one operator served any one route. The names of some of the operators were Croall, Carse, Dougall, Ritchie, Adamson and Atkinson. The colours in which the buses were painted were green, blue, red and orange. I do not have any trace of any of these companies or firms having issued tokens but, like Glasgow, some of them probably did but they were likely destroyed after the company ceased to exist. Tokens were, as I have already mentioned, issued by the Edinburgh Conveyance Co.

A number of tramway companies developed in Edinburgh and the surrounding district. The Edinburgh Street Tramway Co. ran horse-trams in Edinburgh, Leith and Portobello. The first section opened in November 1871. The cars had coloured destination boards and coloured lights at night. This gave an indication of which route they were on. The colours were red, green, red and green and then buff. From 1883 the cars were painted in the colours which represented their routes. The route colours became yellow, white, blue, red and green. The company also ran horse-buses and experimented with steam trams. They were eventually taken over by Leith Corporation Tramways in 1904.

From 1888 Edinburgh Northern Tramways Co. ran cable tramcars until they were taken over by Edinburgh & District Tramways Co. Ltd in 1897. The Northern trams were painted blue with cream panels. The Edinburgh & District Tramways Co. Ltd ran from 1893. They originally used horse-trams and later cable cars. Various plastic tokens were issued by this company. The company was eventually taken over by Edinburgh Corporation Tramways in 1919.

Horse-buses were also run by Edinburgh Street Tramways Co. and Edinburgh Northern Tramways Co.

The Glasgow Tramway & Omnibus Co. also ran horse-buses in Edinburgh and Leith from the 1890s and may have made use of some of their tokens in the east as well as the west.

Edinburgh Corporation Tramways ran cable cars until later the system was electrified. It closed in 1956. The colour scheme was madder, a form of maroon, and white, and this scheme continued with the Corporation motorbuses which are similar to the Lothian buses of the present day.

In the same area of the country Leith Corporation Tramways ran horse and later electric trams from 1904 to 1920 when they were taken over by Edinburgh Corporation Tramways. I have heard rumour that tokens of Leith Corporation Tramways do exist but I do not have any further knowledge or details of this and wonder if this information actually relates to a pass.

Musselburgh & District Electric Light & Traction Co. Ltd ran electric trams from 1904 to 1928.

TWELVE

More Colours

I visited Aberdeen during the Second World War when I was on holiday at the then small village of Portlethan. I well remember the green and cream trams with their many route colours. They had more colours than Glasgow used at that time. They were situated on a band below the upper deck windows and consisted of white, red, yellow, blue, brown and green. From 1949 the colour bands started to disappear. New streamline bogie cars were introduced at about that time and they were painted in green and cream. The buses were also in green and cream. The Corporation issued tokens in many different colours of plastic and the earlier Aberdeen Suburban Tramways issued black penny tokens.

After Aberdeen Corporation Tramways closed down in 1958 an attempt was made to preserve double-deck tram No.73. This tram, which still had open balconies, was taken to the Paisley area and parked in the open but with tarpaulins at each end. Unfortunately it deteriorated through time and eventually had to be scrapped. This was a great pity. Not many years after I saw the Aberdeen tram in Paisley I saw two Glasgow works trams parked at a lay-by near Aberdeen in 1964. These included No.1, the cable laying car, which is now in service at the National Tramway Museum at Crich in Derbyshire.

Aberdeen Corporation tram, numbered 73, waiting for restoration at Paisley. This tram was never restored and was eventually scrapped.

Around the Aberdeen area there were, as I have already mentioned, the tokens issued by the paper mills for the use of their staff on the Great North of Scotland Railway. This was also the railway company which ran the Cruden Bay Tramway, north of Aberdeen. This was a small tramway system which ran to and from Cruden Bay Hotel. It was an electric passenger system which ran from 1899 to 1932 and then, in 1941, by which time it had been taken over by the London & North Eastern Railway Co. for use as a goods transporter. I do not think that tokens were accepted on the tramway.

Dundee was a city which, as a youngster, I did not visit so much but passed through on occasion. I do still remember seeing the trams and buses in their green and white liveries. An earlier colour scheme for the buses was blue and white and until 1961 the green and white also had some orange added. An interesting fact is that although Dundee Corporation motorbuses did not start until 1921 two trolleybuses were used between

Glasgow trams at a lay-by near Aberdeen. They are works cars which have been taken out of service.

1912 and 1914. They were numbered 67 and 68 in the numbering system of the trams. They were sold in 1917 to Halifax Corporation.

Many tokens were issued in the name of the Dundee & District Tramways Co., Dundee City Tramways, Dundee Corporation Transport and Tayside Regional Transport and of course by the horse-bus companies of John M. Robertson, Peter Peebles and Stratton, so Dundee has certainly been one of the cities where transport tokens have generated much interest.

I have touched on colours seen on the transport of the four largest cities. In connection with this, without going into great details of the colours in many other towns in Scotland, I feel that I must mention a few other bus companies which were seen in many parts of the country. The first was W. Alexander & Sons Ltd with their blue and white buses on many routes in Scotland, but it was not their buses but their coaches which most people remember. Not only were these motor coaches blue and cream but on

Glasgow Corporation works car which was formerly passenger car numbered 722, at the lay-by near Aberdeen.

each side was added a 'Bluebird'. It was a very distinctive and pleasant livery. I have memories of going on bus tours to various parts of Scotland in the late 1940s or early 50s. I also remember earlier, during the Second World War, staying with my parents and brother for a weekend at Rosyth and from there we made trips into Dunfermline. I used to particularly enjoy boarding an Alexander's double-deck bus with an open staircase. Most of these buses were I am sure coming to the end of their service life.

Another company which I felt stood out was MacBrayne's. They were based in Glasgow but their buses and coaches ran up and down the west coast of Scotland. Their colour system was very similar to that of Glasgow Corporation motorbuses. They were green and cream but instead of the orange of Glasgow the MacBrayne's buses had red. These colourful vehicles could be seen often connecting with the MacBrayne's steamers and ferries at places like Fort William, Skye and the Kintyre Peninsula.

Another of my holidays took me to Furnace on Loch Fyne and I remember the MacBrayne's buses stopping in the village on their routes down to Ardrishaig, Campbeltown and other towns on the Kintyre Peninsula.

I have not mentioned the town of Perth with its red transport. It is known that at least one plastic token exists of Perth Corporation Transport. Kilmarnock trams were green and tokens are known both for the Corporation and the bus company Western S.M.T., which was based in Kilmarnock. Ayr trams were chocolate and primrose and, of course, tokens were used. Rothesay Tramways Co. originally had a red livery but in the mid-1930s changed to blue, but for tours round the Island of Bute white was used. Later white and black were generally used, followed by red and black during the Second World War and then after the war red and grey. They had many variations of colours and they did issue tokens.

Reverse of ½d token of Perth Corporation Transport Department. (Ref:RB510)

Obverse of ½d token of Perth Corporation Transport Department.

I have written of many colours of trams and buses throughout Scotland but there does not exist a very comprehensive knowledge of the colours used by the horse-bus companies. It may be that more information regarding this will be found some time in the future and, of course, that through time tokens will come to light relating to the services provided by the many other horse-bus companies.

THIRTEEN

Transport Retired

I can remember things relating to transport and tokens dating back to the early 1940s. There will not be many people left who can remember back to the early twentieth century, but we can always visit some of the museums. At the Museum of Transport in Glasgow we may look to the past when we see the old Glasgow horse tram and a horse-bus from the Victorian era. We can also view early electric trams of Glasgow Corporation and even a subway car in a replica station. Also on display are a selection of tokens and passes.

In Aberdeenshire we can visit the Grampian Museum of Transport at Alford. There is exhibited one of the tramcars which ran on the very small system to and from the Cruden Bay Hotel which was run by the Great North of Scotland Railway between the hotel and the railway station. As passes were used by directors of this railway I am sure that at times they would visit this upmarket hotel and use their pass on the trams.

At the museum in Coatbridge you may see and even travel on an old Lanarkshire double-deck tramcar and there are also Glasgow single-deckers.

There are other museums in Scotland and elsewhere, like Crich in Derbyshire, where you can look at and sometimes even travel on the old transport of Scotland.

An old Paisley tram, which was later owned and run by Glasgow Corporation. The tram was in a field near Ballantrae in Ayrshire. It was sold by the Corporation in the 1930s but was eventually scrapped.

Just as I am sure that there are more transport tokens to come to light there may also still be old vehicles to be found. In this connection I know that recently Alan Brotchie came across an old horse-drawn tram of the Edinburgh Street Tramway Co. This was a great find in the Borders of Scotland and it is about to be restored.

As a youngster I often went to Troon on holiday. We, as a family, visited an aunt who lived there. She used to take us in the bus to the village of Dundonald where we went to see the castle and an old ruined house called 'The Auchans'. We often returned by walking through the Dundonald Glen where just before we reached the main road I liked to see an old tramcar which was used as a hut or an outbuilding. It was probably only the body of the tram. As this was in the 1940s it could have been one of the Kilmarnock or Ayr trams. It must have eventually disintegrated.

About twenty years ago I sometimes passed Ballantrae, thirteen miles south of Girvan on the Ayrshire coast, where I used to notice what I thought was a horse-tram in a field, on a hill south of the town. I had seen this tram on occasions for many years before and also an old double-deck bus at a farm nearby. The bus was probably of early 1930s or late 1920s vintage. I do not know what happened to the bus as it ceased to be there years ago.

Eventually I decided one day to make my way to the tram and photograph it. Brian Longworth recently told me that it was actually an old Paisley electric tram, which became owned by Glasgow Corporation after they took over Paisley. It was sold in about the 1930s and used as a summer house at Ballantrae. In the end it was just broken up as it had virtually rotted away. When I saw it the platforms at each end had been removed and so from a distance I had mistaken it for a horse tram. It was a tram that could have seen the use of tokens from both Paisley and Glasgow.

In the catalogue I wish to look at both the description and the value of the Scottish Transport Tokens. As we have seen much of the value is actually in their history and the history of the people who used them in the cities and towns of earlier times.

Catalogue

Listings of the catalogue will include firstly the reference number which I have allocated to a particular token. Secondly I quote the metal or material from which the token is made. The abbreviations for the materials are as follows:

Gold	Au	Silver	Ar
Brass	Brass	Cupro-nickel	CN
Copper	Ae	Bronze	Bronze
Zinc	Zn	Pewter	Pewter
Ivory	Ivory	Plastic/Celluloid	P
Fibre	Fibre		

Next I state the diameter, if the token is round, and the shape and measurements if otherwise. There follows a description of each. Abbreviations of the conditions are as follows:

Unc   Uncirculated (Condition as struck or manufactured)

EF   Extremely Fine (Some slight circulation which may be seen on close inspection)

VF   Very Fine (Traces of wear on raised surfaces, but still with little circulation)

F   Fine (Considerable signs of wear on raised surfaces)

Fair   Fair (Worn but with the main features of the design still distinguishable)

Poor   Poor (Very worn. No value as a collector's piece unless exceedingly rare)

In the listings I have decided to price the tokens in very fine condition and therefore they could command a higher or lower price in relation to them being better or worse than this.

Where a token is of such rarity that only one or a few have been found then I have quoted the price of that particular token according to its state.

The prices in the catalogue are in relation to actual prices obtained or expected to be obtained on the market.

The first part lists Scottish transport tokens in general. Part two relates to transport passes, which tended, in most cases, but not all, to be issued to individuals. It is difficult, sometimes, to have an exact division between tokens and passes. The third section is a list of tokens on the fringe of transportation. These include pay checks used by the Corporations or companies running the vehicles and pay checks of the staff of factories manufacturing different forms of transport. Also listed are tokens used by transport companies for other reasons such as canteen checks. The fourth section quotes some examples of medallions relating to transport.

When referring to tokens having been manufactured in plastic or celluloid this is a general term. In an article by Dr John Tolson he quotes plastic tokens having been made in various materials such as vulcanite (bakelite), vulcanised fibre, celluloid, cellulose acetate, cellulose nitrate and polystyrene (or other polymer). Some combinations of materials have also been used but not all the materials have necessarily been used in Scotland. I have not divided the listed tokens into the various forms of plastic.

With regard to the approximate dates of the issues of some of the plastic tokens I refer to a report by John Rumsley which was supplied to me by Dr John Tolson. The following is quoted in the report:

Glasgow Corporation Tramways:

½d blue issued from 1894, when the Corporation took over the tramways.

1d white issued from 1894.

Glasgow Corporation Transport:

1½d yellow issued from February 1952.

2d black issued from June 1953.

Edinburgh and District Tramways:

½d and 1d tokens issued before 1919.

<u>Edinburgh Corporation Tramways</u>:

In July 1919 the Corporation took over the tramways and continued the use of the above ½*d* and 1*d* tokens and introduced:

1*d* and 1½*d* G.P.O.

1*d* Corporation Gas Department.

1*d* Lighting & Cleansing Department.

1*d* Scholar.

In Edinburgh most ½*d* tokens were withdrawn in March 1941 and in 1949 all tokens were withdrawn except 1*d* white and ½*d* blue (general issues) and 1*d* purple (Scholar). Only these would be accepted by conductors after 1 January 1950. In June 1952 1*d* purple was withdrawn and the 1*d* white was made available to scholars

<u>Kilmarnock Corporation</u>

In the book 'Kilmarnock's Trams and Buses' A.W. Brotchie and R.L. Grieves advise us that celluloid tokens were in use from the start of the tramway system in Kilmarnock in 1904. These were purchased from the National Railway and Tramway Appliance Co. in denominations of ½*d* and 1*d*. Later supplies were obtained from the Hughes Label Co. and then the Corporation itself purchased a press and manufactured their own.

<u>Denominations</u>

As many tokens are in pre-decimal denominations I wish to look at the value relationships before and after 1971.

Before decimalisation:

4 farthings   (¼*d*) = 1 penny (1*d*)

2 halfpennies   (½*d*) = 1 penny (1*d*)

12 pennies   (1*d*) = 1 shilling (1/-)

240 pennies   (1*d*) = 1 pound (£1)

2 shillings   (1/-) = 1 florin (2/-)

20 shillings   (1/-) = 1 pound (£1)

2 shillings & sixpence = halfcrown (2/6)

8 halfcrowns   (2/6) = 1 pound (£1)

Relation of pre-decimal currency to present decimal currency:

Sixpence   (6*d*) = 2½p

One shilling   (1/-) = 5p

One florin   (2/-) = 10p

Four shillings   (4/-) = 20p

Ten shillings   (10/-) = 50p

One pound   (£1) = £1

Before decimalisation in 1971 there were 240*d* to the pound.
After decimalisation there were 100p to the pound.

The letter '*d*' for penny is derived from the old Roman denomination *Denarius* whereas the 'p' of the present system simply stands for 'Penny'.

Token	Material	Size	Inscription	£

ABERDEEN

Token	Material	Size	Inscription	£
RB1	Zn	32mm	Aberdeen, City, Sand check. 'Sand' in centre round 'City of Aberdeen'. Uniface (fair)	25
RB4	Aluminium	33mm	A.P.S. Stoneywood, Aberdeen. Uniface. (Issued by Alex. Pirie & Sons Ltd)	40
RB8	P	23mm	Obverse: Aberdeen Suburban Tramways. Reverse: 1*d* (Black)	15
	P	23mm	Obverse: Aberdeen Corporation Tramways (with City Arms)	
	Reverse:			
RB10	–	–	N.T.C. (Dark Blue) (for use by National Telephone Co. employees)	10
RB11	–	–	N.T.C. (Cream)	10
RB12	–	–	N.T.C. (Cream-coated Orange)	10
RB14	–	–	G.P.O. (Reddish Brown) (for use by General Post Office employees)	8
RB15	–	–	G.P.O. (Maroon)	
RB16	–	–	G.P.O. (Dark Red)	8
RB17	–	–	G.P.O. (Light Red)	8
RB20	–	–	B/ ½*d* (Reddish Brown) (for use by the Blind)	7
RB21	–	–	B/ ½*d* (Dark Brown)	7
RB22	–	–	B (White)	7
RB25	–	–	P (Lemon) (for use by the Police)	7

Token	Material	Size	Inscription	£
RB26	–	–	P (Yellow)	7
RB28	–	–	1*d* On Military Duty (Pink)	7
RB29	–	–	½*d* On Military Duty (Transparent)	7
RB32	–	–	½*d* (Blue)	5
RB33	–	–	½*d* (Blue Centre between Dark Blue Slices)	7
RB34	–	–	½*d* (Dark Blue)	5
RB36	–	–	¾*d* (Dark Green)	6
RB37	–	–	¾*d* (Light Blue)	6
RB38	–	–	¾*d* (Dark Blue)	6
RB40	–	–	1*d* (Bluish Green)	4
RB41	–	–	1*d* (Light Blue)	4
RB42	–	–	1*d* (Blue)	4
RB44	–	–	1½*d* (Light Pink)	4
RB45	–	–	1½*d* (Pink)	4
RB46	–	–	1½*d* (Purple)	4
RB48	–	–	2*d* (White)	4
–	P	23mm	Obverse: Aberdeen Corporation Transport (with City Arms)	
			Reverse:	
RB50	–	–	1*d* (Light Blue)	2
RB51	–	–	1½*d* (Red)	5
RB52	–	–	2*d* (White)	5
RB53	–	–	3*d* (Lemon)	2
RB54	–	–	3*d* (Yellow)	2
RB56	–	–	4*d* (Brown)	3
RB57	–	–	4*d* (Dark Brown)	3
RB58	–	–	5*d* (Red)	3
RB59	–	–	6*d* (Dark Green)	3
RB60	–	–	9*d* (Pink)	3

Token	Material	Size	Inscription	£
RB62	–	–	A.C.T. (Green)	2
RB63	–	–	A.C.T. (Beige)	2
RB64	–	–	A.C.T. (Light Orange)	2
–	P	22mm	Obverse: Grampian Transport (With a thistle at the 'I' of 'Grampian')	
			Reverse:	
RB67	–	–	1p (Yellow)	1
RB68	–	23mm	2p (Orange)	1
–	P	22mm	Obverse: Grampian Regional Transport (Arms)	
			Reverse:	
RB69	–	–	G.R.T. (Orange) (for 10p fare)	1
RB70	–	–	5p (Black)	1
RB71	–	–	10p (Red)	1
RB72	–	–	10p (Light Maroon)	1
RB73	–	–	15p (Blue)	1
RB74	–	–	20p (Grey)	1

AYR

Token	Material	Size	Inscription	£
–	P	23mm	Obverse: Ayr Corporation Tramways (with Town Arms)	
			Reverse:	
RB77	–	–	½d (Pink centre between dark red slices)	20
RB78	–	–	½d (Red) (Thick)	15
RB79	–	–	½d (Red) (Thin)	15
RB80	–	–	½d (Dark Blue)	15
RB81	–	–	1d (White)	15
RB82	–	–	1½d (Dark Blue)	15

Token	Material	Size	Inscription	£

CLYDEBANK

| RB84 | Ae | 29mm | Obverse: U.C.B.S.Clydebank Renfrew Ferry 4*d* No. (Stamped Numbers) | |
| – | – | Pierced | Reverse: Blank | 45 |

CULTER (ABERDEENSHIRE)

	Brass		CMP COY LTD – Culter and Aberdeen (for use by employees of Culter Mills Paper Coy Ltd)	
RB86	–	33mm	Uniface (with narrow letters on obverse)	35
RB87	–	31mm	Uniface (with wide letters on obverse)	30
–	–	–	CMP COY LTD – Culter and Cults	
RB88	–	31mm	Uniface	30

DUNDEE

RB90	Bronze	Oval	Obverse: John M. Robertson 23 Perth Road & Meadowside 2*d*	35
		28x19mm.	Reverse: Town Omnibus (depicting Horse-drawn Omnibus)	
RB91	Pewter	Oval	Obverse: (wording as previous token)	25
–	–	28x19mm	Reverse: (as previous token)	
RB94	Brass	Oblong	(clipped corners) Obverse: Peter Peebles Dundee Perth Road	35

Token	Material	Size	Inscription	£
—	—	23x16mm	Reverse: City Bus 2*d*	
RB96	Ae	Oval	Obverse: Stratton 2*d*	35
		29x21mm	Reverse: East End Bus	
RB98	Brass	38mm	Obverse: Tay Ferries No.	
			(with number stamped on obverse)	80
—	—	—	Uniface	
RB100	Brass	Oval	Obverse: Dundee & District	
			Tramways Coy 1*d*	30
—	—	32x20mm	Uniface	
RB101	Brass	27mm	Obverse: Dundee & District	
			Tramways Coy 2*d*	30
—	—	—	Uniface	
RB102	Brass	Oblong	Obverse: Dundee & District	
			Tramways Coy 3*d*	30
—	—	32x20mm	Uniface	
—	P	23mm	Obverse: Dundee City	
			Tramways (with City Arms)	
—	—	—	Reverse:	
RB105	—	—	½*d* (Yellow)	2
RB106	—	—	½*d* (Light Green)	5
RB107	—	—	½*d* (Bluish Green)	5
RB108	—	—	½*d* (Light Blue)	5
RB109	—	—	½*d* (Blue)	5
RB110	—	—	½*d* (Dark Blue)	5
RB111	—	—	½*d* (Black)	6
RB114	—	—	1*d* (White)	2
RB115	—	—	1*d* (White coated Orange)	6
RB116	—	—	1*d* (Pink coated Dark Rose)	6
RB117	—	—	1*d* (Light Pink coated Brown)	6
RB118	—	—	1*d* (Orange)	5
RB120	—	—	1*d* (Light Red)	5

Token	Material	Size	Inscription	£
RB121	–	–	1*d* (Red)	5
RB122	–	–	1*d* (Dark Red)	5
RB123	–	–	1*d* (Light Brown)	5
RB124	–	–	1*d* (Brown)	5
RB125	–	–	1*d* (Dark Grey)	
–	P	23mm	Obverse: (City Arms) Reverse: Dundee Corporation Transport with denomination) as follows:	
RB130	–	–	1*d* (White)	2
RB131	–	–	1½*d* (Light Blue)	4
RB132	–	–	2*d* (Dark Brown)	2
RB133	–	–	3*d* (Green)	2
RB134	–	–	3*d* (Olive)	2
RB135	–	–	6*d* (Pink)	2
–	P	23mm	Obverse: Tayside Regional Transport (with Arms) Reverse – Tayside Regional Transport (with denomination) as follows:	
RB138	–	–	3p (Orange)	2
RB139	–	–	4p (Red)	2
RB140	–	–	5p (Blue)	2
RB141	–	–	10p (Yellow)	3

DUNFERMLINE

Token	Material	Size	Inscription	£
RB150	Brass	30mm	Obverse: Dunf. & Dist. Trys. Co. Employee 2*d* Reverse (Stamped Numbers)	50

Token	Material	Size	Inscription	£
RB153	P	23mm	Obverse: Dunfermline and District Tramways G.S. Reverse 2*d* (Red)	20

EDINBURGH

Token	Material	Size	Inscription	£
–	Bronze	30mm	Obverse – Union Canal Time Ticket (pierced)	
RB160	–	–	1st Stage One Hour & 55 MINes. (Stamped W)	100
RB161	–	–	1st Stage One Hour & 55 MINes. (Stamped E)	100
RB162	–	–	1st Stage One Hour & 45 MINes. (Stamped W)	100
RB163	–	–	1st Stage One Hour & 45 MINes. (Stamped E)	100
RB164	–	–	2d Stage One Hour & 45 MINes. (Stamped W)	100
RB165	–	–	2d Stage One Hour & 45 MINes. (Stamped E)	100
RB166	–	–	2d Stage One Hour & 35 MINes. (Stamped W)	100
RB167	–	–	2d Stage One Hour & 35 MINes. (Stamped E)	100
RB168	–	–	3d Stage One Hour & 45 MINes. (Stamped W)	100
RB169	–	–	3d Stage One Hour & 45 MINes. (Stamped E)	100
RB170	–	–	3d Stage One Hour & 35 MINes. (Stamped W)	100
RB171	–	–	3d Stage One Hour & 35 MINes. (Stamped E)	100

Token	Material	Size	Inscription	£
RB172	–	–	4th Stage One Hour & 55 MINes. (Stamped W)	100
RB173	–	–	4th Stage One Hour & 55 MINes. (Stamped E)	100
RB174	–	–	4th Stage One Hour & 45 MINes. (Stamped W)	100
RB175	–	–	4th Stage One Hour & 45 MINes. (Stamped E)	100
RB177	–		4th Stage One Hour & 45 MINes. (Stamped E) (This may be a pattern or trial piece) Extremely fine (unpierced)	150

An unpierced token of ref No. RB171 has been found and therefore this would rank with No. RB177. They may be trial pieces or unissued tokens.

There is also a token of ref No. RB171 which has the '*d*' of '3*d*' struck twice. Once the right way up and once overstruck upside down.

In connection with these Union Canal Time Tickets I quote from *Catalogue of World Ferry, Ship, and Canal Transpotation Tokens and Passes*, compiled by Kenneth E. Smith and Kirk S. Smith:

These beautiful tokens were apparently used in the early 1800s. These tokens are all either Rarity 10, one known, or Rarity 9, two known. E is for the trip east on the boat. W is for the trip west on the boat. It is probable that the first two tokens of each stage were the first to be used and later the travel time was reduced by 10 minutes per stage and the other tokens with reduced time replaced them.

Token	Material	Size	Inscription	£
RB180	Brass	29mm	Obverse: Fife & Midlothian Ferries Co. No. (with numbers stamped) Uniface	30
RB182	Brass	35mm	Obverse: London & Edinburgh Shipping Co. Ltd Uniface	30
RB185	Ae	25mm	Obverse: Edinburgh Conveyance Co. 1*d*	45
			Reverse: Tollcross to Register Office	
RB186	Ae	25mm	Obverse: Edinburgh Conveyance Co. 2*d*	45
			Reverse: Tollcross to Register Office	
RB190	P	23mm	Obverse: Edinburgh & District Tramways Co. Ltd – School	12
			Reverse: 1*d* (Red)	
–	P	23mm	Obverse: Edinburgh & District Tramways Co. Ltd – Exchange	
RB194	–	–	Reverse: ½*d* (Green)	10
RB195	–	–	Reverse: ½*d* (Blue)	10
RB196	–	–	Reverse: 1*d* (White)	8
RB198	P	23mm	Obverse: Edinburgh & District Tramways Co. Ltd Gas Commission 1*d*	10
			Reverse: for use 6a.m. to 6p.m., not available on Sundays, 6a.m. to 2p.m. on Saturdays (Red)	
–	P	23mm	Obverse: Edinburgh Corporation Tramways (Arms)	
RB199	–	–	Reverse: P.O. 1*d* (Post Office) (Dark Green)	5
RB200	–	–	Reverse: G.P.O. 1½*d* (General Post Office) (Yellow)	5

Token	Material	Size	Inscription	£
RB201	–	–	Reverse: ½d (Blue)	4
RB202	–	–	Reverse: 1d (White)	4
RB203	–	–	Reverse: 1½d (Dark Blue)	4
RB205	–	–	Reverse: 1d (White) Edinburgh Corporation Tramways	4
–	P	23mm	Obverse: Edinburgh Corporation Tramways Gas Commission 1d	
RB207	–	–	Reverse: for use 6a.m. to 6p.m., not available on Sundays, 6a.m. to 2p.m. on Saturdays (Red)	5
–	P	23mm	Obverse: Edinburgh Corporation Tramways 1d	
RB209	–	–	Reverse: for use 6a.m. to 6p.m., not available on Sundays, 6a.m. to 2p.m. on Saturdays (Dark Brown)	4
RB210	–	–	Reverse: for use 6a.m. to 6p.m., not available on Sundays, 6a.m. to 2p.m. on Saturdays (Black)	4
RB211	P	23mm	Obverse: Edinburgh Corporation Tramways 1d Scholar Reverse: Available any distance on one car between 8a.m. to 6p.m. weekdays, 8a.m. to 2p.m. Saturdays (Violet)	4
RB212	P	23mm	Obverse: Edinburgh Corporation Transport Gas Department 1d Reverse: for use 6a.m. to 6p.m.,	3

Token	Material	Size	Inscription	£
			not available on Sundays, 6a.m. to 2p.m. on Saturdays (Red)	
–	P	23mm	Obverse: Edinburgh Corporation Transport 1*d*	
RB213	–	–	Reverse: for use 6a.m. to 6p.m., not available on Sundays, 6am to 2p.m. on Saturdays (Brown)	3
RB214	–	–	For use 6a.m. to 6p.m., not available on Sundays, 6a.m. to 2p.m. on Saturdays (Dark Brown)	3
–	P	23mm	Obverse: Edinburgh Corporation Transport 1*d* Scholar	
RB215	–	–	Reverse: Edinburgh Corporation Transport (with City Arms) (Violet)	3
–	P	23mm	Obverse: Edinburgh Corporation Transport (with City Arms)	
RB219	–	–	Reverse: G.P.O. 1*d* (Green) (Thick)	3
RB220	–	–	Reverse: G.P.O. 1*d* (Green) (Thin)	3
RB221	–	–	Reverse: G.P.O. 1*d* (Dark Green)	3
–	P	22mm	Obverse: Edinburgh Corporation Transport (with City Arms)	
RB222	–	–	Reverse: Edinburgh Corporation Transport 1*d* (with no dot after *d* & reverse lettering small) Beige	2
–	P	23mm	Obverse: Edinburgh Corporation Transport (with City Arms)	
RB225	–	–	Reverse: Edinburgh Corporation Transport – 1*d* (White)	2
RB226	–	21mm	Reverse: Edinburgh Corporation Transport – 1½*d* (Blue)	2

Token	Material	Size	Inscription	£
RB227	–	23mm	Reverse – Edinburgh Corporation Transport – 1½d (Dark Blue)	2
RB228	–	–	Reverse: Edinburgh Corporation Transport – 2d (Red)	2
RB229	–	–	Reverse: Edinburgh Corporation Transport – 3d (Lemon)	2
RB230	–	–	Reverse: Edinburgh Corporation Transport – 3d (Yellow)	2
RB231			Reverse: Edinburgh Corporation Transport – 4d (Green)	2
–	P	22mm	Obverse: Edinburgh Corporation Transport (with City Arms)	
RB232	–	–	Reverse: 1d (White)	2
–	P	23mm	Obverse: Edinburgh Corporation Transport (with City Arms)	
RB235	–	–	Reverse: 5d (Black)	2
RB236	–	–	Reverse: Edinburgh Corporation Transport 6d (Brown)	2
–	P	23mm	Obverse: Edinburgh Corporation Transport 6d	
RB240	–	–	Reverse: 2½p (Brown) (used October 1970 to 1978)	2
RB241	–	–	Reverse: 2½p (Brown) (6 overstruck on a partially removed reverse 6)	3
–	P	23mm	Obverse: Edinburgh Corporation Transport (with City Arms)	
RB245	–	–	Reverse: 2½p (Brown)	2
RB246	–	–	Reverse: 3p (Pink)	2

Token	Material	Size	Inscription	£
RB247	–	–	Reverse: 4p (Light Blue)	2
RB248	–	–	Reverse: 5p (Lemon)	2
–	P	23mm	Obverse: Lothian Regional Transport (with Arms)	
RB250	–	–	Reverse: 4p (Light Blue) (used from 1977)	1
RB251	–	–	Reverse: 5p (Yellow)	1
RB252	–	–	Reverse: 10p (Green) (used from 1976)	1
RB254	–	–	Reverse: 20p (White) (used from 1984)	1
–	P	23mm	Obverse: Lothian LRT	
RB255	–	–	Reverse: 5p (Yellow)	1
RB257	–	–	Reverse: 10p (Green)	1
RB259	–	–	Reverse: 25p (Blue)	1
RB260	–	–	Reverse: 50p (Red)	
–	Brass	–	Obverse: Lothian Region Transport LTR Lothian	
RB265	–	–	Reverse: Value as advertised – A	2

FALKIRK

Token	Material	Size	Inscription	£
RB270	White Metal	23mm	Obverse: FDTC (interwoven letter) (issued by Falkirk District Tramways Co.) Uniface	30
–	Brass	33mm	Obverse: W. Alexander & Sons Ltd – Falkirk	
RB272	–	–	4*d* (on Obverse)	25

Token	Material	Size	Inscription	£
RB273	–	–	2½ (on Obverse)	25
RB274	–	32mm	3*d* (on Obverse)	25
RB275	Brass	31mm	Obverse: A.M.S. 2/– (Issued by Alexander Motor Service) Uniface	30
RB276	Brass	31mm	Obverse: A.M.S. 3/– Uniface	30

GLASGOW

Token	Material	Size	Inscription	£
	Brass	–	Obverse: The Glasgow and Partick Omnibus Coy Limited G & P O Co.	
RB280	–	21mm	Reverse: Half Fare (in wreath)	40
RB281	–	25mm	Reverse: Inside (in wreath)	50
RB282	–	Oval 31x24mm	Reverse: Outside (in wreath)	50
–	Ae	Oval 25x20mm	Obverse: MacEwens City Omnibus	25
RB285	–	–	Reverse: 2*d*	
	White Metal	20mm	Obverse: Wylie & Lochhead 28 Argyle Street	
RB286	–	–	Reverse: 2*d*	150
RB287	–	24mm	Reverse: 4*d*	150
	White Metal	20mm	Obverse: Wylie & Lochhead 58 Union Street	
RB288	–	–	Reverse: Pass Ticket	150
RB289	–	24mm	Reverse: Pass Ticket	150

Token	Material	Size	Inscription	£

(Information relating to these Wylie and Lochhead tokens regarding the position of the wording relates to the sightings of about forty years ago. It may be that the addresses are on the reverse and probably included 'Glasgow')

Token	Material	Size	Inscription	£
	Ae	Oblong	Obverse: James Walker Funeral Undertaker	
		28x13mm	4*d* Tontine and 104 & 108 West Nile St.	
RB290	–	–	Reverse: Post & Job	
			Master Glasgow (Horse)	
			(Fine Condition)	400
	Ae	Oval	Obverse: Andrew Menzies 10	
		28x18mm	Argyle St. & 110 London St. 2*d*	
RB294	–	–	Reverse: City Omnibus	
			(Horse-drawn Omnibus)	30
RB295	–	–	Reverse: as above except	
			counterstamped with a 'P' over	
			the 2*d* to denote a penny fare	35
	Ae	Oblong	Obverse: Andrew Menzies	
		25x19mm	Funeral Undertaker and Jobmaster	
RB296	–	–	Reverse: City Omnibus	
			Fare 2½*d*. Jany Glasgow 1856	60
RB297	–	–	Reverse: as above except ½ of 2½*d*	
			obliterated and token	
			counterstamped with an	
			emblem like a 'Y'	60
	Ae	Oval	Obverse: Andrew Menzies Funeral	
		28x18mm	Undertaker Coach Proprietor	
			Glasgow	

Token	Material	Size	Inscription	£
RB298	–	–	Reverse: City Omnibus fare 2*d*. May 1859 Andrew Menzies Glasgow	30
	Brass	Oval 20x14mm	Obverse: Crosshill Omnibus Co. 1*d*	
RB301	–	–	Reverse: (Horse-drawn Omnibus)	60
RB302	–	–	Obverse: Crosshill Omnibus Co. 2*d* Reverse: (Horse-drawn Omnibus)	60
	Brass	Round 33mm	Obverse: Glasgow Tramway Co. Ltd (Round Central Design★)	
RB305	–	–	Reverse: Blank	40
	Brass	Round 25mm	Obverse: The Glasgow Tramway & Omnibus Co. Ltd Sand Ticket	
RB306	–	–	Reverse: Blank	45
	Ae	Oval 28x19mm	Obverse: The Glasgow Tramway & Omnibus Co. Ltd	
RB308	–	–	Reverse: Letter Carrier in Uniform	45
	Ae	Oblong 28x19mm	Obverse: The Glasgow Tramway & Omnibus Co. Ltd	
RB309	–	–	Reverse: Telegraph Boy in Uniform	45
	Brass	Round 30mm	Obverse: Cowan & Co. – Ferry	

Token	Material	Size	Inscription	£
RB312	–	–	Reverse: (Blank)	25
	Pewter	Round 30mm	Obverse: Cowan & Co. – Ferry	
RB313	–	–	Reverse: (Blank) (There are thick and thin varieties of these tokens)	20
	Brass	Round 29mm	Obverse: M/M Ferry	
RB315	–	–	Reverse: (Blank)	20
	Pewter	Round 29mm	Obverse: M/M Ferry	
RB316	–	–	Reverse: (Blank)	18
	Pewter	Oblong 27x20mm	Obverse: Glasgow and Paisley Canal Co.	
RB320	–	–	Reverse: (Blank)	80
	White Metal	Oblong 27x20mm	Obverse: Glasgow and Paisley Canal Co.	
RB321	–	–	Reverse: (Blank)	90
	Brass	Round 25mm	Obverse: Clyde Navigation	
RB325	–	–	Reverse: Govan Ferry and Wharf	20
	Brass	Round 32mm	Obverse: Clyde Navigation (Anchor and Chain) (Graining on Edge)	

Token	Material	Size	Inscription	£
RB326	–	–	Reverse: Two Penny Ferries Ticket	15
	Brass	Round 26mm	Obverse: Clyde Navigation (Anchor and Chain) (Graining on Edge)	
RB327	–	–	Reverse: Half Penny Ferries Ticket	5
RB328	–	–	Reverse: Half Penny Ferries Ticket (with six pointed stars)	5
	Zinc-plated Steel	Round 26mm	Obverse: Clyde Navigation (Anchor and Chain) (Graining on Edge)	
RB329	–	–	Reverse: Half Penny Ferries Ticket	5
	Brass	Round 37mm	Obverse: Glasgow & Liverpool Royal Steam Packet Co.	
RB332	–	–	Reverse: Deck Glasgow to Liverpool – if this ticket be lost the fare must be paid again	25
	White Metal	Round 40mm	Obverse: Glasgow and Liverpool Steam Shipping Co. Cabin	
RB334	–	–	Reverse: (Steamship sailing left)	130
RB335	–	–	Reverse: (Variety – as above but countermarked with 'U' above 'cabin' and number below)	130
	White Metal	Octolobe 32mm	Obverse: R.D.S. Ltd Ferry	
RB338	–	–	Reverse (Blank)	20

Token	Material	Size	Inscription	£
RB340	Brass –	Round 36mm –	Obverse: Orient Co. Ltd (Stamped with number) (Holed as issued) Reverse: Price of ticket to replace this sixpence (stamped with number)	25
RB343	Brass –	Round 32mm –	Obverse: Caledonian Steam Packet Co. Ltd Workman's check Reverse: Breakfast Dinner or Supper	60
RB344	Brass –	Oval 25x21mm –	Obverse: Glasgow Corporation Tramways ½d Reverse: Blind	15
RB345	Brass –	Oblong 24x20mm –	Obverse: Glasgow Corporation Tramways 1d Reverse: Blind	15
RB350 RB351	P –	Round 25mm –	Obverse: Glasgow Subway Railway Reverse: ½d (Blue) Reverse: 1d (White)	12 12
RB355 RB356	P – –	Round 23mm – –	Obverse: The Glasgow Tramway & Omnibus Co. Ltd (Tramcar) Reverse: Tramway Check One Penny Fare (Arms) (Red) Reverse: Tramway Check One Penny Fare (Arms) (Pinkish Red)	10 10

Token	Material	Size	Inscription	£
	White Metal	Oval 29x20mm	Obverse: Glasgow and South Western Railway Co.	
RB360	–	–	Reverse: (Blank)	50
	White Metal	Oblong 27x20mm	Obverse: Glasgow & South Western Railway Co. Parcels	
RB361	–	–	Reverse: (Blank)	50
	Brass	Oblong (39x26mm)	Obverse: Jas. Shaw Contractor	
RB365	–	–	Reverse: (Blank)	20
	P	23mm	Obverse: Glasgow Corporation Tramways (City Arms)	
RB370	–	–	½d (White)	3
RB371	–	–	½d (Dark Red)	5
RB372★★★	–	–	½d (Light Green)	4
RB373★★★	–	–	½d (Green)	4
RB374	–	–	½d (Dark Green) (very thick)	6
RB375	–	–	½d (Light Blue)	3
RB376	–	–	½d (Blue)	3
RB377		22mm	½d (Dark Blue)	3
RB378	–	–	½d (Very Dark Blue)	3
RB379	–	–	½d (Very Dark Blue) (very thick)	4

Note ref ★★★RB372/373   These are quoted in Smiths' catalogue but I have not seen any other reference to them so possibly they are variations in colour of the Blue or Light Blue ones.

Token	Material	Size	Inscription	£
	P	22mm	Obverse: Glasgow Corporation Tramways (City Arms)	
	Reverse:			
RB380	Fibre	–	½d (Black)	3
RB384	P	–	1d (White)	3
RB385	Fibre	–	1d (Pinkish Grey)	4
RB386	P	–	1d (Dark Blue) (thick)	4
RB390	–	–	2 stage token (Lemon)	10
RB391	–	–	2 stage token (Black)	10
RB392	–	–	2 stage token (Black)(Pierced)	8
RB393	Fibre	24mm	2 stage token (Reddish Brown)	4
RB394	–	23mm	2 stage token (Reddish Brown)	4
RB395	P	22mm	2 stage token (Reddish Brown) (thick)	4
RB396	–	–	2 stage token (Maroon)	1
RB397	–	–	2 stage token (Dark Red)	1
RB398			2 stage token (Dark Red) (Fish in Coat of Arms angled at about 45 degrees.)	3
RB400	–	–	2 stage token (Bright Red)	8
	P	23mm	Obverse: Glasgow Corporation Transport (City Arms)	
RB405	–	–	Reverse: J.I.C. ½d (Yellow)	5
RB406	–	–	Reverse: J.I.C. 1d (Orange)	5
RB407	–	–	Reverse: J.I.C. 2d (Black)	5
RB409	–	24mm	Reverse: ½d (Green)	4
RB410	–	–	Reverse: ½d (Dark Green)	2
RB411	–	22mm	Reverse: ½d (Light Green)	2
RB412	–	–	Reverse: ½d (Light Blue)	2
RB415	–	23mm	Reverse: 1d (White)	2
RB416	–	–	Reverse: 1d (White)(with small city arms)	2

Token	Material	Size	Inscription	£
RB418	–	–	Reverse: 1½d (Yellow)	2
RB419	–	–	Reverse: 2d (Black)	2
RB420	–	–	Reverse: 2d (Black)(with small city arms)	2
RB421	–	–	Reverse: 3d (Red)	2
RB422	–	–	Reverse: 4d (Pink)	2
RB423	–	–	Reverse: 6d/2½p (Purple)	2
RB425	–	–	Reverse: 1p (Green)	2
RB426	–	–	Reverse: 3p (Orange)	2
	P	23mm	Obverse: G.G.P.T.E. (with large GG in the centre)	
RB430	–	–	Reverse: 5p (Black)	2
RB431	–	–	Reverse: 10p (White)	2
	Brass	30mm	Obverse: First Glasgow (Emblem of First Group) valid for one single journey	
RB435	–	–	Reverse: Same as obverse (This token had a value of up to £1 25p from 28 August 1998)	5
	White Metal	Oval 23x13mm	Obverse: South Portland Street Suspension Bridge 1853	
RB440	–	–	Reverse: (City Arms)	30
RB442	P	30mm	Obverse: Logo of First Group printed on orange plastic tokens. (These were only issued on 6 August 2005. They were given to people attending a disco to	

Token	Material	Size	Inscription	£
			enable them to use the night service buses) The reverse is blank.	3

GREENOCK

Token	Material	Size	Inscription	£
	Ae	23mm	Obverse: Murray Greenock (Horse-drawn Omnibus)	
RB450	–	–	Reverse: Fare Two Pence (in wreath of Roses)	50
	Brass	22mm	Obverse: James Orr Railway Coach Office Greenock	
RB452	–	–	Reverse: (Horse-drawn Omnibus)	45
	Brass	25mm	Obverse: Dd McFarlane Coach Proprietor 2d & Funeral Undertaker	
RB454	–	–	Reverse: 25 West Blackfall St. Greenock May 1866 2d	40

(This token was issued by Donald McFarlane and his address should read 25 West Blackhall St.)

Token	Material	Size	Inscription	£
	P	23mm	Obverse: G (Crown) R	
RB455	–	–	Reverse: G.P.O. (Blue) (I have not had sight of this token but quote from Smiths' catalogue)	10
–	–	23mm	Obverse: G. & P.G. Tramway Coy (Round Magnet and Wheel Emblem) (Issued by Greenock & Port Glasgow Tramway Co.)	

Token	Material	Size	Inscription	£
RB456	P	–	Reverse: ½d (White)	6
RB457	Fibre	–	Reverse: ½d (Black)	6
RB458	Fibre	–	Reverse: ½d (Olive Green)	6
RB459	P	–	Reverse: 1d (Light Blue)	6
RB460	Fibre	–	Reverse: 1d (Brown)	6
RB461	P	–	Reverse: 1d (Light Blue) (Large letters on obverse)	7
RB462	Brass	39mm	Obverse: Cabin to Greenock Reverse: (Steamboat)	30

HELENSBURGH

Token	Material	Size	Inscription	£
RB463	Ae	Oval 29x21mm	Obverse: Helensburgh and Gareloch Steamers Reverse: Return Ticket Available only on the day of issue or the day following	55
RB464	Ae	24mm	Reverse: (Same as RB463)	50
RB465	Ae	Square 23mm	Reverse: (Same as RB463)	50
RB466	Ae	Oblong 25x16mm	Reverse: (Same as RB463)	55
RB467	White Metal	Oval 29x21mm	Reverse: (Same as RB463) – (Pattern)	60
RB468	Pewter	Oval 30x21mm	Reverse: (Brockage)	50

KILMARNOCK

Token	Material	Size	Inscription	£
	P	23mm	Obverse: Kilmarnock Corporation Tramways	

Token	Material	Size	Inscription	£
			(Town Arms)	
RB469	–	–	Reverse: ½d (White)	15
RB470	–	–	Reverse: 1d (Red)	15
RB471	–	–	Reverse: 1d (Maroon)	15
	P	22mm	Obverse: Western S.M.T. Co. Ltd	
RB473	–	–	Reverse: ½d (White)	16
RB474	–	–	Reverse: 1d (Red)	16

KIRKCALDY

Token	Material	Size	Inscription	£
	Ae	37mm	Obverse: Kirkcaldy or Dysart Ferry Cabin No. (Numbers)	
RB476	–	–	Reverse: (Blank) (Stamped 'B' on the obverse)	30
RB477	–	–	Reverse: (Blank) (Stamped 'St.G' on the obverse)	30
	Ae	37mm	Obverse: Kirkcaldy or Dysart Ferry Steerage No. (Numbers)	
RB478	–	–	Reverse: (Blank) (Stamped 'B' on the obverse)	30
RB479	–	–	Reverse: (Blank) (Stamped 'St.G' on the obverse)	30
	Ae	Square 32mm	Obverse: Kirkcaldy or Dysart Ferry Cabin No. (Numbers)	
RB480	–	–	Reverse: (Blank) (Stamped 'St.G' on the obverse)	30

Token	Material	Size	Inscription	£

LEITH

Token	Material	Size	Inscription	£
RB481	Bronze	Oblong 53x39mm	Leith and Newhaven Ferry (Stamped Queen D in two lines)	25

LEVEN

Token	Material	Size	Inscription	£
	Ae	37mm	Obverse: Leven or Largo Ferry Cabin No. (Numbers)	
RB482	–	–	Reverse: (Blank) (Stamped 'B' on the obverse)	30
RB483	–	–	Reverse: (Blank) (Stamped 'St.G' on the obverse)	30
	Ae	37mm	Obverse: Leven or Largo Ferry Steerage No. (Numbers)	
RB484	–	–	Reverse: (Blank) (Stamped 'B' on the obverse)	30
RB485	–	–	Reverse: (Blank) (Stamped 'St.G' on the obverse)	30

MOTHERWELL

Token	Material	Size	Inscription	£
	P	23mm	Obverse: The Lanarkshire Tramways Co. Motherwell (Statio Bene Fide Carinas) (Double-Deck Tramcar 1903)	
RB486	–	–	Reverse: ½d (White between Brown slices)	10
RB487	–	–	Reverse: ½d (White)	8

Token	Material	Size	Inscription	£
RB488	–	–	Reverse: 1*d* (Orange)	8
RB489	–	–	Reverse: 1*d* (Red)	8
RB490	–	–	Reverse: 1*d* (Maroon)	8
RB491	–	–	Reverse: 1½*d* (Light Blue)	8
RB492	–	–	Reverse: 1½*d* (Dark Blue)	8
	P	24mm	Obverse: Central S.M.T. Co. Ltd (with denomination) same on reverse	
RB494	–	–	Reverse: ½*d* (Black printing on White)	15
RB495	–	25mm	Reverse: 1*d* (Black printing on Cream)	15
RB496	–	–	Reverse: 3*d* (Red printing on Cream)	15
RB497	–	24mm	Reverse: 1/– (Colours not known)	15

PAISLEY

Token	Material	Size	Inscription	£
	Aluminium	Hexagonal 25mm	Obverse: Paisley District Tramways Co. (Arms)	
RB500	–	–	Reverse: ½*d*	25
	Brass	29mm	Obverse: S.G. & Co. No. (Numbers) Paisley (These tokens were issued by Spain, Gibb & Co.)	
RB502	–	–	Reverse: Blank – (Stamped E.L. on Obverse Refers to Empty Lorry)	30
RB503	–	–	Reverse: Blank – (Stamped L.L.	

Token	Material	Size	Inscription	£
			on Obverse Refers to Loaded Lorry)	30
RB505	Brass	Oblong 39x26mm Pierced	Obverse: W. Cumming - Reverse: Blank	25
RB506	Pewter	Oblong 39x26mm. Pierced	Obverse: W. Cumming – Reverse: Blank	20

PERTH

RB510	P	22mm	Obverse: Perth Corporation Transport Department – Reverse: ½d (Green)	30

(The only known example of this token is held by the Perth Museum)

ROTHESAY

RB518	Zn	26mm	Obverse: P.O. Telegraphs Messengers tokens (around a Crown) Reverse: same as Obverse but counterstamped RX	15
RB520	P	23mm	Obverse: Rothesay Reverse: E (crown) R G.P.O. (Red)	12
RB522	Fibre	23mm	Obverse: G.P.O. Reverse: 1½d (Black)	10

Token	Material	Size	Inscription	£

RUTHERGLEN

| RB525 | White Metal | 26x17mm Octagonal | Obverse: Glasgow Rutherglen ★ Omnibus (issued by Rutherglen Omnibus Co.) Reverse: (Blank) | 250 |

WEMYSS

	P	23mm	Obverse: The Wemyss & District Tramways Co. Ltd (Arms)	
RB530	–	–	Reverse: 1*d* (White)	8
RB531	–	–	Reverse: 1½*d* (Green)	8

Token	Material	Size	Inscription	£

GLASGOW UNDERGROUND 'PARK AND RIDE' TOKENS

Token	Material	Size	Inscription	£
RB550	Brass	22.5mm	Obverse: GGPTE (round a) U. Reverse: Car Park	5
RB551	Brass	22.5mm	Obverse: SPTE (round a) U. Reverse: Car Park (The 'E' of SPTE is reversed)	5
RB552	Brass	22.5mm	Obverse: SPTE (round a) U. Reverse: Car Park	6
RB553	Brass	24.5mm	Obverse: Strathclyde Transport (round a large thin) U Reverse: Bridge Street Park and Ride	10
RB554	Brass	24.5mm	Obverse: Strathclyde Transport (round a large thin) U Reverse: West Street Car Park	10
RB555	Brass	24.5mm	Obverse: SPTE (across the token) Reverse: K/B (The 'K/B' represents Kelvinbridge Subway Station	10
RB556	Brass	24.5mm	Obverse: Strathclyde Transport (round a large thin) U Reverse: Park and Ride, Park and Ride	4
RB557	Brass	24.5mm	Obverse: ASL Reverse: (Blank)	

Token	Material	Size	Inscription	£

TRANSPORT PASSES

EDINBURGH

Token	Material	Size	Inscription	£
RB600	Brass	29mm	Obverse: Edinburgh & Dalkeith (round) J. Young Reverse: Railway Coach	35
RB610	Ar	32mm	Obverse S.M.T. Associated Companies (around a thistle) (with integral loop at the top) Reverse: Free Pass (above a naming panel)	220
RB615	Brass	33mm	Edinburgh Street Tramways (Numbers, Wreath & Pierced)	35

GLASGOW

Token	Material	Size	Inscription	£
RB620	Ar	Oval 28x23mm	Obverse: Glasgow Corporation Tramways (on a blue enamel background) (The lettering is round the Glasgow Coat of Arms) (with integral loop at the top) Reverse: Permit No.	40

ABERDEEN

Token	Material	Size	Inscription	£
–	Aluminium	42mm	Obverse: Aberdeen Corporation Tramways (City Arms)	
RB625	–	–	Reverse: No. (Numbers) Employee's pass available only when on duty (Thick & Thin)	50

Token	Material	Size	Inscription	£

ARDROSSAN

RB630 — Ar — — — Ardrossan Railway (engraved in old English characters)

(Taken from *Tickets & Passes of Great Britain and Ireland* by W.J. Davis & A.W. Waters) — 80

THE CLYDE

RB640 — Au — Oval 28x18mm — Obverse–Caledonian Steam Packet Co Limited (and pennant of the company) (pierced as issued, for suspension) Reverse: J. Conacher Esq. — 260

ARBROATH & FORFAR

RB650 — Ar — — — The Arbroath & Forfar Railway Co. (upon a buckled garter and engraved in centre) Free/Ticket

(Taken from *Tickets & Passes of Great Britain and Ireland* by W.J. Davis and A.W. Waters) — 200

CENTRAL SCOTLAND

RB660 — Ar — — — Obverse: Scottish Central Railway Free Ticket. Reverse: Joseph Locke ESQre, Civil Engineer (Engraved on both sides)

Token	Material	Size	Inscription	£

(Taken from *Tickets & Passes of Great Britain and Ireland* by W.J. Davis & A.W. Waters) 200

GREAT NORTHERN RAILWAY

| RB670 | Ivory | Oval 30x22mm | Obverse: Great Northern Railway Free Pass Reverse: Samuel Mendal Esq. Director M.S & L. Ry Co. (Pierced as issued) | 220 |

KENMORE

| RB680 | Brass | Oval 25x15mm | Obverse: Loch Tay Steamers (around 'BB' with the second 'B' reversed & all below a crown) (with an integral Boar's Head at the top and a loop for suspension) Reverse: Free Pass (with a number in the centre) | 95 |

| RB690 | Brass | Oval 28x15mm | Obverse: Loch Tay Steamers (around 'BB' with the second 'B' reversed & all below a crown) (with an integral Boar's Head at the top and a loop for suspension) Reverse: Free Pass (at the left) T. Mosley (at the right) (number in the centre) | 95 |

Token	Material	Size	Inscription	£

WEMYSS

| RB700 | Brass | 42mm | Obverse: The Wemyss and District Tramways Co. Ltd (with the Wemyss coat of arms) Reverse: Service Pass (together with a number) | |

(The pass is made of two thin pieces of metal joined together)   90

FALKIRK

| RB710 | Steel | Round 61mm | W. Alexander & Sons Ltd Duty Pass No. – (Pierced) (Enamelled) | 20 |
| RB720 | Steel | Oblong 118x56mm | W. Alexander & Sons Ltd Duty Pass No. – This duty pass valid only on vehicles operated by the company. It must be returned immediately to the issuing office when the holder has completed his or her journey. (White stove enamel & blue letters with the number put on with rubber stamp) Reverse: Blank black stove enamel. | 20 |

Token	Material	Size	Inscription	£

FRINGE TOKENS

(Related to Transport but not usually used for conveyance)

WORKS CHECKS or TOKENS

DUMFRIES

RB790   Brass   27mm   Arrol Johnston Uniface Check
(Stamped with numbers)
(Car Manufacturer)   10

DUNDEE

RB800   Brass   Oval 45x26mm
Dundee Shipbuilders Co. Ltd (Uniface) 10

EDINBURGH

RB810   CN   Oval   Peebles Motor Co. Ltd Uniface
33x20mm   Check (Stamped with numbers)   8

GLASGOW

RB820   Brass Diamond   35x44mm
Obverse: Glasgow Corporation
(Pierced)   Tramways (City Arms)
Reverse: (Stamped various
abbreviations for the depot name.)
(Stamped with a number relating to the employee and stamped 'DR'
to denote a driver)   15

Token	Material	Size	Inscription	£
RB830	Brass	39mm (Pierced)	Obverse: Glasgow Corporation Tramways (City Arms) Reverse: (Stamped various abbreviations for the depot name.)	

(Stamped with a number relating to the employee and stamped 'CR' to denote a conductor) — 18

Token	Material	Size	Inscription	£
RB840	Brass	Oval 28x40mm (Pierced)	Obverse: Glasgow Corporation Tramways (City Arms) Reverse: (Stamped with a number relating to the employee and 'Mains' or 'Dep' and sometimes an abbreviation for the depot)	15
RB850	Brass	35mm	William Beardmore & Co. Ltd – Aviation – (Uniface – stamped with a number.)	

(Beardmore were also famous for the manufacture of taxi cabs) — 10

Token	Material	Size	Inscription	£
RB860	Brass	34mm	North British Locomotive Co. Queen's Park (Uniface Stamped with a number.)	10
RB870	Brass	32mm	London & Scottish Car Co. Glasgow Garage (with a letter and number on the reverse)	8
RB880	–	29x23mm	Rolls-Royce (with letters and number stamped on reverse)	8
RB890	–	Oval 51x26mm	The Clyde Shipping Co. (Bracteate check depicting SS *Caledonia*)	8
RB900	Zn	Rect 39x29mm	Clydebank Shipyard (with letters and number stamped on reverse)	10

Token	Material	Size	Inscription	£
RB910	Lead	Rect 29x20mm	Robert Napier & Sons (with letters and number stamped on reverse)	10
RB920	Brass	32mm	Barclay Curle & Co. (with the wording 'Whiteinch' and numbers stamped)	10

PORT GLASGOW

Token	Material	Size	Inscription	£
RB924	Brass	33mm	M M & Co. (Stamped with numbers) – (Pierced as issued) (Murdoch Murray & Co., Shipbuilders, Brown Street, Port Glasgow)	8

OTHER WORKS CHECKS

Token	Material	Size	Inscription	£
RB930	Brass	Hexagonal 32x33mm	London Midland & Scottish Railway (Stamped with number) (Uniface)	5
RB940	Galvanised Iron	38mm	London Midland & Scottish Railway (Stamped with number) (Uniface)	5

CANTEEN TOKENS

Token	Material	Size	Inscription	£
RB960	Brass	28mm	Glasgow Locomotive Works (with 3½d in the centre)	25
RB961	Brass	33mm	Glasgow Locomotive Works (with 4d ½ in the centre)	25

Token	Material	Size	Inscription	£
RB965	Brass	25mm	Harland & Wolff Canteen Token H1½dW (uniface)	10
RB970	Brass	Octagonal 30mm	Wylie & Lochhead (of Glasgow) (with the wording 'Welfare' and '3d'	25

(This token was probably issued in connection with the large store in Buchanan Street in Glasgow, rather than be related to the horse-buses.)

OTHER FRINGE TOKENS

Token	Material	Size	Inscription	£
RB980	Brass		Carlaw Cars (issued by Carlaw Cars in Paisley for car wash)	7
RB1000		Brass	Hexagonal Mallaig Railway Workmen's Club (with a number stamped between the wording 'Member's Ticket') Reverse: (A star design in scores across the brass)	20

MEDALLIONS RELATED TO TRANSPORT

RB1100   White Metal 49mm
(A railway medallion depicting on the obverse: Great Viaduct over the valley of the Almond near Edinburgh.) Picture of Viaduct – to commemorate the opening of the Edinburgh and Glasgow Railway, 18 February 1842. On the reverse: (Entrance to the Glasgow Railway Station and Tunnel Pictured – Published by S. Woolfield, Royal Exchange Square, Glasgow.

Token	**Material**	**Size**	**Inscription**	**£**

RB1120 White Metal

Bridge Medallion with the obverse: (View of Bridge) Bridge of Dunkeld, ex length 685 ft. Breadth (sic)27 and centre Arch is 90 feet. Reverse: built by the most noble John Duke of Atholl. Expence above £30,000. Founded 24 June 1805 and opened 7 November 1808.

(Quote from *Tickets & Passes of Great Britain and Ireland* by W.J. Davis & A.W. Waters)

RB1140 Ar   —

Dunvegan Castle Steam Ship – Obverse: (view of ship within a lifebelt) inscribed sports on board Castle Cos Steamer. (All shown upon an anchor with olive branches at side)

        Reverse: 2nd Prize Dunvegan Castle (Engraved)

(Quote from *Tickets & Passes of Great Britain and Ireland* by W.J. Davis & A.W. Waters)

RB1160 Gilt Bronze   27mm

Ring for suspension – The George Bennie Rail plane on a monorail above a steam locomotive. Below is the wording 'Opening June 1930' – (The Rail Plane was at Milngavie Glasgow)

Some details relating to Fringe Tokens and Medallions have been taken from Auction and other lists and, therefore, the exact details may, in some cases, vary from those quoted.

In relation to the Transport Passes and, even more so, the Fringe tokens and medallions those quoted are only a small number in relation to the total which probably exist.

Bibliography

Books

Stage-Coach to John O' Groats by Leslie Gardiner. (Hollis & Carter, 1961)

The Second City by C.A. Oakley. (Blackie & Son Ltd)

The Last Tram by C.A. Oakley. (Corporation of the City of Glasgow (Transport Department) 1962)

Tickets & Passes of Great Britain and Ireland by W.J. Davis & A.W. Waters.

The Manchester Carriage and Tramway Company by Edward Gray. (1977)

The Aberdeen District Tramways by M.J. Mitchell & I.A. Souter. (N.B. Traction, Dundee)

Kilmarnock Trams and Buses by A.W. Brotchie and R.L. Grieves. (N.B. Traction, Dundee)

The Tramways of Ayr by Ronald W. Brash. (N.B. Traction, Dundee)

Stirling's Trams & Buses by A.W. Brotchie. (N.B. Traction, Dundee)

Tramways of the Tay Valley by Alan W. Brotchie. (A Dundee Museum and Art Gallery publication)

Edinburgh's Transport: The Early Years by D.L.G. Hunter. (The Mercat Press, Edinburgh)

Glasgow Subway 1896-1977 by Paul J. Kelly and M.J.D. Willsher. (Light Railway Transport League)

I Belong to Glasgow: The Human History of the Glasgow Underground by Gordon Casely and Bill Hamilton. (Nexus Press Ltd)

Old Killin, Kenmore and Loch Tay by Bernard Byron. (Stenlake Publishing)

Steamers of the Tay by Ian Brodie. (Stenlake Publishing)

Tramways of Scotland by Ian L. Cormack (M.A. Published by the Scottish Tramway Museum Society)

Old Glasgow: The Place, The People, 1880 by A. Macgeorge.

Catalogue of World Transportation Tokens and Passes Except North America (1967) by Kenneth E. Smith.

Catalogue of World Horsecar, Horseomnibus, Streetcar and Bus Transporting Tokens Except North America (1990) by Kenneth E. Smith and Kirk S. Smith.

Catalogue of World Ferry, Ship and Canal Transportation Tokens and Passes (1981) by Kenneth E. Smith and Kirk S. Smith. (American Vecturist Association)

<u>Newspapers</u>
The Glasgow Herald / The Herald

<u>Other Sources</u>
Scottish Tramlines/Transport of the Scottish Tramway & Transport Museum Society.

The Auction Catalogues of Simmons Gallery, 53 Lamb's Conduit Street, London

The Coin, Token and Banknote sales lists of Format, 18/19 Bennetts Hill, Birmingham.

The sales lists of Alan Judd.

The manuscripts on 'The Glasgow Horse Buses and Trams' by M. Morton Hunter.

The Auction Catalogues of Dix, Noonan, Webb of 1 Old Bond Street, London

Visit our website and discover thousands of other History Press books. **www.thehistorypress.co.uk**

The History Press